SPE the CTRAL TIDE

true ghost stories
of the u.s. navy

eric mills

SPECTRAL the TIDE

true ghost stories
of the u.s. navy

Eric G. Mills

NAVAL INSTITUTE PRESS
Annapolis, Maryland

Naval Institute Press
291 Wood Road
Annapolis, MD 21402

Library of Congress Cataloging-in-Publication Data
Mills, Eric, 1959–
 The spectral tide : true ghost stories of the U.S. Navy / Eric Mills.
  p. cm.
 Includes bibliographical references.
 ISBN 978-1-59114-495-3 (alk. paper)
 1. Ghosts—United States—Anecdotes. 2. Parapsychology—United States—
Anecdotes. 3. United States. Navy—History—Anecdotes. 4. United States—
History, Naval—Anecdotes. 5. Seafaring life—United States—History—Anec-
dotes. I. Title.
 BF1472.U6M55 2009
 133.10973—dc22

                              2009027762

Printed in the United States of America on acid-free paper ∞

15 14 13 12 11 10 09   9 8 7 6 5 4 3 2
First printing

gift   10/16

To Mom
great teacher, great storyteller, always an inspiration

Contents

Preface   xi

Acknowledgments   xiii

Translucent Sails on Lonely Seas   1

Manifestations of Captain Jones   11

Spirits in the Timbers   17

The Flaming Ghost-Ship of Mahone Bay   29

Twin Phantoms of the Mysterious Lake   35

A Hero Remains Forever   45

A Fatal, Perfidious Brig   55

The Annapolis Anomaly   70

Haunted Bases and Other Places   78

Battleships of the Dead   89

Echoes of Infamy   100

Blue-Eyed Charlie and Shadow Ed   106

Brothers to the End, and Beyond   117

A Hornet's Nest of Hauntings   123

Of Hangars and Their Hangers-on   132

Hell's Flight Deck   138

For Those in Peril on the Sea   142

Source Notes   145

Bibliography   157

Into the caverns of the deep
Go phantom ships, where phantom faces
Peer in the dark; not even sleep
Can blind their eyes; arm interlaces
With kelp and salty fin; feet tread
The somber currents of the dead.

Into dark caverns, deep and strange,
Go specter-ships, with specter-men;
Fathoms are theirs, and theirs the range
Of hemispheres beyond the ken
Of human mind and human heart—
A country on a wider chart.

—Marguerite Janvrin Adams

Have you ever been on a haunted ship? Did you ever wake up to find a clammy hand clawing your shoulder, or hear a mysterious voice from nowhere bidding you arise? Did you ever see a shadowy, creepy thing gliding across the deck and coming between you and the person you were talking to? Did your hair ever rise and your skin make "gooseflesh" at rumblings or thuds or thumps or harrowing groans where living beings were not? You have not? Then you are no sailor.

—*Washington Post*, February 3, 1907

Preface

Death has a disturbing way of leaving its mark upon a location; the more violent and untimely the death, the more prevalent its hovering essence. Some are blessed with an inability to detect such unpleasantness; they are as impervious to death's signals as to a sound-wave pitched too highly for their auditory limitations. But those burdened with an innate sensitivity to spectral lingerings know well the grim, unwanted sensation: You enter a room, and your intuition recoils from some time-dimmed act of mutilation and gore that has left its psychic scar. A hallway where an axe-murder occurred will be tainted thereafter with a repugnant aura; a basement where a child was strangled will never lose its unremittant sense of raw horror. But you don't know about the axe murder, you've never heard of the demented strangulation—the details come later, part of the attempt to expiate the wafting dread that knocked you back. Death imparts its mystic stain upon the place where it occurred, and we grapple with such an unsettling imponderable with what feeble articulation we can summon, and we call it a haunting.

Can there be any location more conducive to such morbid echoes than a warship? By inherent purpose it is a space where death comes screaming and suddenly. In harm's way the good die young, but even when the air is not thick with fire and shrapnel, mere daily routine can be fraught with risk on a ship of war. If a house can reverberate with the terror of a decades-old murder, imagine the aural aftershocks of that one death multiplied tenfold, a hundredfold—warships are vessels that carry such voluminous supernatural baggage in their holds.

From its scrappy upstart beginnings to its emergence as the most powerful sea force the world has ever known, the United States Navy has sailed audaciously into the thick of the fray. A litany of victories and a legacy of valor have generated a superfluity of hauntings as their phantasmal side-effects. Those who have served in the Navy tend to be familiar with some ghost stories; many are familiar with more than just the stories, but the spirits that spawned the stories as well. From the Old Navy's heroic days of broadsides and boarding parties to the ultramodern Navy of now, the ghost-lore stretches in a mystical continuum, an epic time line of the eerie and the unexplained. The Navy's ghostly history is presented here with an open mind to the unknown possibilities of a boundless universe. In dealing with matters of the spirit-realm, the degree of veracity one is willing to grant such accounts inevitably must vary from individual to individual; nonetheless these stories, these admittedly bizarre reports, do exist, regardless of whether or not one dares to believe them. They are recounted in this narrative with an eye to unearthing the actual history that lies beneath the supernatural mystery, to gleaning the overlap between the historical and the paranormal.

Here, then, is a saga of phantom ships and ghostly crews, of cursed craft, ectoplasmic captains, and banshee-howls in the oceanic night—the haunted history of the U.S. Navy.

Acknowledgments

On the quest for these spectral sea stories I benefited greatly from the helpful assistance of many. My heartfelt thanks go to the staffs of the Library of Congress, the National Archives, thew U.S. Naval Academy's Nimitz Library, the Stephen Decatur House and Museum, the USS *Lexington*, the USS *North Carolina*, the John Paul Jones House and Museum, the Freeport Historical Society, the Portsmouth (Maine) Public Library, and the California Room of the San Diego Public Library. Let me also thank my friend Lt. Cdr. Thomas J. Cutler, USN (Ret.), of the Naval Institute Press for his enthusiasm for the project; the talented production and design departments of the press also have my gratitude. Great thanks as well to Mindy Connor, a gifted editor who really got into the spirit of the proceedings. Above all, I thank my wife and family for their unflagging encouragement and support while I delved into matters arcane and mysterious.

Translucent Sails on Lonely Seas

The mightiest ship is but a speck on the vast, primordial ocean. From the dimly remembered seafaring days of canvas and oar to this prideful age of nuclear-powered steel behemoths, fragile humans have sallied forth on their frail vessels, braving the blue planet's far watery reaches, venturing out beyond that distant line where heaven meets the waves.

Many fleets under many flags have gone there, are there now. But there is among them one fleet—the most dreaded of all—that sails for all time, a cumulative fleet of all ages and all lands: the fleet of the dead, the unfortunate ones who never made it back—never, that is, to our concrete dimensional realm. They are out there forever, sad and lost, hollow-eyed wraiths on rotted deck planks, their translucent sails traversing lonely seas. Occasionally, by virtue of some unfathomable metaphysical confluence, they cross paths with us. And the modern sailor who bears witness to a ship from the fleet of the dead feels a sudden disquieting chill, a flash of dread as ancient as the sea itself.

Such an encounter was fated for the USS *Langley* in 1937. The U.S. Navy's first aircraft carrier was on a course for Coco Solo, Panama, when sailors aboard her beheld an unearthly vision in the pale glow of dawn: there, on the horizon, a sailing ship—fully rigged, all canvas unfurled and bulging with wind—speeding straight toward them. The news spread fast through the steel-hulled giant, and crewmen scrambled on deck for a view. As the beautiful old vessel raced ever closer and the sun rose in the sky, the officers and men of the *Langley* stared dumbfounded as the sailing ship dissolved into nothingness.

The *Langley*, they speculated, had just had a run-in with the fabled *Flying Dutchman*. The centuries-old phantom had been reappearing with some frequency in recent years; a whaling ship spotted her in 1911, as did a Royal Navy ship in 1923, as would German admiral Karl Dönitz in 1939. The *Langley*'s encounter with the *Dutchman* came on the cusp of a period that would see a strange uptick in spectral-ship sightings, an awakening of dormant wraiths as the seas roiled with global strife.

The destroyer USS *Kennison* soon thereafter experienced a pair of phantom-ship encounters while plying the waters off the California coast. Approaching San Francisco Harbor in November 1942 she nearly collided with a two-masted sailing ship—timbers rotting, sails ragged, crumbling deck deserted, helm unmanned. But the *Kennison*'s radar screen was blank. The mystery ship was there . . . but not there. More strangeness came the destroyer's way in April 1943 as she was making for her home port of San Diego. A Liberty ship appeared off the starboard bow and then vanished without a trace, befuddling multiple witnesses and refusing to register on the perfectly functioning radar screen.

"As a witness who saw one ship, and heard the other . . . I believe that the explanation for the shadow fleet that sails in the tradition of the *Flying Dutchman* lies in the area of psychic phenomena," stated Howard Brisbane of the *Kennison*. "Reports of these apparitions have been made by generations of responsible men."

But why then? Why such a resurgence? The world in those dark days was in the throes of the largest, deadliest conflict in its long and bloody history. The Grim Reaper's harvest during World War II was the most horrendous of all time. It was as if all the tragedy, all the carnage, all the death stirred up echoes of the waterlogged dead of old, summoning the spectral tide to rise. And while enigmatic Pacific wraiths crossed the *Kennison*'s bow, on another ocean in the same war, another famed ghost ship made its first reappearance in many years.

There lies a cold and rock-rimmed bay where the North American coast juts eastward from its predominantly north–south course, a bay that by virtue of its geography is the site of the closest American port city to Europe. As such, Casco Bay, Maine, found itself at the nexus of events as the Battle of the Atlantic raged, with the fate of Great Britain, the European continent, and the free world hanging in the balance. This wave-tossed New England district, so steeped in maritime lore, had become busier and more vital than ever before—the most important American seaport of World War II. From Portland Harbor to Harpswell Neck, from Cape Elizabeth to Cape Small, old Casco was in full martial mode, bristling with gun emplacements, bunkers, barracks, lookout towers, and great deadly ships of steel—the combined sea might of the Royal Navy, the Royal Canadian Navy, the U.S. Navy, and the U.S. Coast Guard. Here was a key embarkation point for the beleaguered convoys that were the very life's blood of war-scarred Britain. A crucial oil pipeline from Montreal fed the Allied shipping that braved forth through chill northern seas where deadly German U-boat wolf packs prowled.

And sometimes the wolves came in threateningly close, lurking among the hundreds of windswept islands in the offshore maze. So it was that those who manned the coastal guns and scrutinized the water in August 1942 felt their nerves on the keenest edge, for just that June one of the dreaded German U-boats had been sighted right out there in Casco Bay.

A fog thick as chowder enveloped all in an eerie aura as the howling radar alarm suddenly jarred the afternoon stillness, heralding one of the most bizarre unexplained occurrences in the annals of World War II. Blipping its way ominously across the Navy radar screen, violating the defensive perimeter, some ocean-borne intruder was surging brazenly toward the innermost zone of restriction. Sirens screamed, men ran to battle stations, ships swarmed, and guns zeroed in.

Two clandestine lovers were lying in an amorous tangle on the water's edge at Punkin Nubb when they heard the sirens. An artillery shell exploded, raining rock shards, right alongside them. The man's first, fleeting guilty thought was of the woman's husband, of jealous wrath writ large, but he peered out into the fog and saw big doings. A Royal Navy vessel had charged forth, guns blazing, from Cumberland Cove, and her U.S. Navy allies were in on the chase as well, all of them converging on a floating trespasser.

And then, out of the mist, the lovers saw the offending vessel materialize. It wasn't a U-boat. It wasn't German at all. It wasn't even of this era. It was a wooden sailing craft of yesteryear, coming right past Punkin Nubb with two modern navies in hot pursuit. As it came closer, they could see the ship's name carved into the wood:

Dash—Freeport.

There she sailed, close by and plain as day—a ship that had sunk 127 years earlier.

* * *

Rarely was a vessel more aptly named, for the *Dash* was truly one of the swiftest craft afloat during her heyday in the War of 1812, and one of the greatest of all the privateers to sail for America in that war. It was said of her, "She never suffered defeat, never attacked an enemy's ship in vain, was never injured by a hostile shot and knew no equal in speed."

Seward Porter's shipyard, founded at Porter's Landing in 1782, was the birthplace of the storied brig. When she was launched in 1813, the *Dash* represented the apotheosis of the shipwright's art. In designing her the brothers Porter had pioneered a methodology hitherto unused along the Maine coast, for rather than fashioning her lines by naked-eye reckoning, the standard technique then, the Porters had built the *Dash* from a ship's-hull model—the first such known in Maine history (it survives to this day at the Freeport Historical Society). Her sleek design prefigured the clippers that would rise to prominence a generation hence. What she lacked in cargo space she made up for in exceptional speed. Initially rigged as a topsail schooner, she was a merchantman designed to run the British blockade, which she did with resounding success.

The *Dash* commenced her career with a smuggler's run to San Domingo, unloading New England goods for a tidy profit and loading up with coffee for the return run. It was then that she ran afoul of a British man-of-war. A cannon barked the order to halt; sails unfurling, the *Dash* raced away. The British warship could not match her speed, and the *Dash* came into Portland battered (a damaged foremast) but unbowed. The legend was born.

Off came the foremast and on went a stouter spar and square sails, and the topsail schooner metamorphosed into a hermaphrodite brig—a vessel with a brazen abundance of canvas and a concomitantly greater aptitude for speed. Out she ventured again, to be chased again, and to escape the British guns again—and to realize riches and renown again on her second voyage. The legend was growing apace with the elusive blockade-runner's exploits.

But even a bolder destiny was the *Dash*'s lot. "Fortune favors the bold," Virgil said, and the ship's owners realized that there was more to be gained—both in booty and in service to the cause of independence—by setting sail as sanctioned sea robbers, pirates in the name of young America. So it was that on September 13, 1814, the owners received their letter of marque, a commission from President James Madison that officially sanctioned the *Dash* to act as a privateer. The infant U.S. Navy had but a handful of fighting ships to face the unparalleled might of the British sea force, and the service of privateering vessels such as the *Dash* was vital to the war's outcome. The *Dash* and her privateering sisters were in effect the auxiliary U.S. Navy, and they exemplified the courage, daring, intrepidity, and rock-solid Yankee sea skill of the new nation. The War of 1812 was history's shining moment for American privateers, and the *Dash* was one of the most successful of them all.

Newly fitted out with two 18-pound cannon and a 32-pound pivot gun, she headed out for fighting and plunder. Her first prize was a British cruiser, which she hauled into port along with a profitable cargo. Soon she was chasing down and giving battle to HMS *Lacedemonian*. Not only did the *Dash* capture the British warship, she also reclaimed an American ship the Royal Navy ship had earlier bested and captured. On her subsequent voyage, a British frigate and schooner attempted to gang up on the *Dash*, but the wily American managed to separate the schooner from the frigate and then gave the outfoxed schooner a thorough thrashing.

Soon she was the scourge of the English sea-lanes, the terror that accompanied each British merchant ship's forays on the main. The *Dash* was the particular pride of the Casco coast; seagoing lads from Portland, Harpswell, and Freeport vied for the honor of a billet aboard the audacious plunder ship. Twenty-four-year-old John Porter, bold young scion of the shipbuilding family that owned the *Dash*, assumed the captaincy and wasted no time, taking two prize ships his first week out. He liberated the American privateer *Armistice* from the clutches of the brig HMS *Pactolus* and increased his capture yield by taking a pair of sloops and a brig. Three months at sea and half a dozen prizes: with brave Porter at the helm, the *Dash* reached the height of her renown—or the nadir of her notoriety, depending on the colors one sailed beneath.

Porter continued to venture forth, totaling fifteen captures during the autumn of 1814. And through it all, the *Dash* never lost a man; nor did any of the crew suffer wounds or injury of any kind. The word ran among the dockside villages that truly this was a good-luck ship. Then 1814 turned into 1815, and a bleak January day saw the deck of the *Dash* aswarm with busy crewmen eager to set sail anew, greedy for more plunder and greater fame.

It was a tragedy of those bygone days that news traveled slowly; and it was tragic, too, that this famed ship with a spotless record of success would soon besmirch it with an unnecessary undertaking. For the sturdy sailors of

Portland did not realize, as they outfitted the *Dash* on that chill Maine day in the middle of January 1815, that the Treaty of Ghent had been signed on Christmas Eve 1814. The war was already over. Like Andrew Jackson and his fierce fighters to the south who won a brilliant but ex post facto victory at the Battle of New Orleans that selfsame January, the *Dash* was embarking unknowingly on a moot adventure. It was fated to be her last.

Sails a'luffing, pacing up and down Portland Harbor, straining impatiently like a champion at the starting gate, the *Dash* was cleared for sea with all crew in attendance—except for young Captain Porter. He was still at home in the embrace of sweet Lois, his wife of a few fleeting months. The newlyweds held each other as if they knew it was their last chance ever to do so. The sudden boom of the signal cannon interrupted the precious moment. Captain Porter ignored the insistent summons, and still the two savored their togetherness. The signal cannon roared a second time, and he knew he had to go.

His crew was in high spirits, for along with the promise of another gainful cruise there was the more immediate thrill of a race with another privateer. The newly built *Champlain* stood by in the harbor waiting to challenge the legendary *Dash* in an outward-bound race. The pair of them sped southward out of Portland Harbor. The upstart *Champlain* proved no match for the famously fast *Dash*, which by the next morning had vastly outdistanced her impertinent challenger. The *Champlain*'s crew watched the *Dash* grow ever smaller in the distance.

And then the gale came, an almost supernatural blow bringing high winds and driving snow. And in the blinding sting of whiteness, those on the *Champlain* lost sight of the *Dash* and never saw her again.

Nor did anyone else. Through ensuing days, weeks, and months of anguish and eroding hopes, the families and friends of the *Dash*'s sixty lost crewmen yearned for some sign of their fate. But the great *Dash* had vanished without a trace.

It was said that Lois Porter intuited the worst a couple of nights after the *Dash* had departed. As the foul storm descended on the coast and the ill wind blew with all the harshness of midwinter's dark despair, Lois heard a crashing noise in an empty room. She went into the unoccupied portion of the house cautiously, and there she found the source of the disturbance. The raging wind had worked its way within, dislodging a mantelpiece tile and shattering it on the floor. The destroyed tile had borne a scriptural passage. Lois picked up the broken pieces, knowing as she did so that she would never see her beloved husband again and that the *Dash* was never going to return to Casco Bay.

No one ever determined what befell the great privateer. She might have broken up on the dreaded Georges Shoals, toward which she was headed when the gale caught her in its teeth. It was a viable guess, but just that—a guess, a stab at a question that none among the living could answer. As one of the *Dash*'s chroniclers noted, "Never a piece of wreckage reached the shore. No floating spar nor splintered boat ever appeared to offer its mute testimony."

The *Dash* had doubtless met her doom, but it soon became evident that she still hovered in this realm—that she still haunted the waves, trapped for eternity in a Möbius loop of unrequited homesickness. After several months had passed, she returned from oblivion for the first time, emerging in the fogbound gloaming. A local sea harvester named Simon Bibber was pulling in a good haul just off Punkin Nubb when a strange ship emerged from the gray-white swirl, shorebound under full sail. And yet there was no wind.

When the mystery craft hove within thirty feet of the stunned fisherman, her nameplate was clearly visible: *Dash—Freeport.*

Simon Bibber watched in shock as the lost ship passed by, bound for her place of origin. He put muscle to oar and hastened into Freeport. But the prodigal ship was not there when he arrived. Bibber found old Mort Collins by the docks and told him of sighting the *Dash*. Mort reacted with bemused skepticism. He regarded Simon Bibber as a man deranged, and so Bibber himself began to believe, until another *Dash* sighting occurred. This time it was Roscoe Moulton who bore witness to the ectoplasmic entity. He had been off Crab Island when "she flew past me like a whirlwind, and they warn't a breath of air stirring, thick o' fog and flat-arse calm," Moulton avowed. "I seen her!"

And so, too, did others as time passed. Numerous sightings occurred from Eagle Island to Pound o' Tea. When the fog settled in and the wind was silent, she'd heave into view, sailing fast "no matter which way the wind was blowing or the tide flowing," her forlorn crew gathered at the rail peering longingly for the home they could not reach. As more living souls attested to the recurring phenomenon, its existence, however inexplicable, became accepted as fact. The roster of believers in the unbelievable came to include all seventeen crewmen of the schooner *Betty Macomber*, returning to port with a bounteous haul of cod when there came the *Dash*, ghostly, close, careening past with all speed. One nineteenth-century chronicler of the strange reported that "be it calm or storm, in-come or ebb of tide, the ship holds her way until she almost touches shore."

The intermittent spectral sightings entered the mainstream of New England lore and inspired the celebrated American poet John Greenleaf Whittier to pen "The Dead Ship of Harpswell":

> What flecks the outer gray beyond
> The sundown's golden trail?
> The white flash of a sea-bird's wing,
> Or gleam of slanting sail?
> Let young eyes watch from Neck and Point,
> And sea-worn elders pray,—
> The ghost of what was once a ship
> Is sailing up the bay!

Many and varied were the *Dash* sightings, yet one common thread goes to the essential melancholy of this particular otherworldly presence: the poor *Dash* can never quite make it all the way home. As soon as she is almost there, back seaward she must drift again. Some say that she heads back out to sea stern-first.

> For never comes the ship to port,
> Howe'er the breeze may be;
> Just when she nears the waiting shore
> She drifts again to sea.
> No tack of sail, nor turn of helm,
> Nor sheer of veering side;
> Stern-fore she drives to sea and night,
> Against the wind and tide.

In the wake of some of the initial sightings a theory about the *Dash*'s appearance quickly came to predominate: her coming was a harbinger of death—whenever the ghostly sails reappeared, a family member (be it immediate family, extended family, or, as time passed, a descendant) of one of the *Dash*'s doomed crew was going to die.

Some home amid yon birchen trees
Shall drape its door with woe;
And slowly where the Dead Ship sails,
The burial boat shall row!

The *Dash* sightings became more sporadic as the decades wore on (although how many sightings have gone unreported lest the reporter be accused of insanity one can only conjecture), but they never ceased entirely. A summer guest at Harpswell House in the 1880s was taking the air on the verandah when he suddenly spied her, a beautiful, if unsettling, image of billowing sails. He hailed others to come quickly and see, and in the moment it took to do so, poof, the *Dash* had disappeared yet again.

How ironic that this famed participant in a long-ago war in which the United States and Great Britain were grim foes should reappear during World War II, when the two nations were allies and friends; and that this ghost ship should run the gauntlet between their two navies. How interesting, how resonant of the past, that the ship that fired on the fast-moving ghost of the *Dash* in 1942 was a Royal Navy ship, a descendant of that same mighty navy that fired on the *Dash* during her existence on this physical plane. The ponderings such mystical oddities evoke are fodder for the student of karma and the philosopher; they must remain beyond the purview of this more earth-bound accounting of events. Suffice it to say that the local Lothario who bore witness to the *Dash*'s ghost, and almost bore the brunt of a British artillery shell, loaded his lady love onto his boat and attempted the row away from the commotion with all deliberate speed. He was apprehended and interrogated by U.S. Navy officials, who, rendered incredulous by the paranormal details of his statement, ultimately felt compelled to bury the whole inexplicable affair amid the war's massive bureaucratic paperwork. Other area residents had backed his story rather than dispelling his ghost ship assertions, and the Navy decided that shelving the whole insane incident was the sanest course. The modern world, in all its grim, gray, steel-hulled seriousness, had just had a brief glimpse into the abyss of the unknowable, and had experienced the same unsettling pang that prompted the poet's unanswerable question:

What weary doom of baffled quest,
Thou sad sea-ghost, is thine?

The spectral essence of the *Dash* harkens to a past when the Navy was in its formative years, when its fighting ships were all too few and privateers helped even the odds. The Navy may have been in its infancy back then, but here was an infant with a heroic father: a father who has a haunting presence—literally—to this day.

Manifestations of Captain Jones

You may speak of gallant Conyngham, of the prizes he took and the havoc he wreaked. You may sing the praises of bold John Barry, of his audacious victories from Newfoundland to Florida. You may pen fanciful wardroom ballads extolling intrepid Lambert Wickes, terror of the English Channel and the Irish coast. But of all the heroic figures who set sail to fight for American independence, one name alone still echoes like thunder across the rolling waves: John Paul Jones.

Jones, the first to raise the American flag on a ship-of-war. Jones, the raider of St. Mary's Isle, the champion of Carrickfergus, the sea god of Flamborough. Jones, whose thirst for action was captured in unequivocating declarations: "I wish to have no connection with any ship that does not sail fast, for I intend to go in harm's way." And, "I have not yet begun to fight!" John Paul Jones—words inscribed in marble offer apt summation at his hallowed sarcophagus: "He gave our Navy its earliest traditions of heroism and victory."

His was an adventurous, restless, wandering soul—and there is evidence that it remains so to this day.

John Paul Jones' apparition is of a category not bound to one location (the spirit of a murder victim, by contrast, tends to remain rooted to the scene of the grisly crime). Like the specters of other historical figures—Anne Boleyn and Abraham Lincoln likewise fall into this classification—the spectral manifestations of Captain Jones have been witnessed in more than one spot.

Geographically dispersed hauntings are not so surprising in the light of the widely wandering life Jones led. But the mystery becomes: Why these haunted sites and not others? If his ghost is adrift, why does he not revisit his birthplace, the small cottage on the windy Scottish coast that still stands in monument to him today? Why has he not deemed to appear in the colonial Fredericksburg, Virginia, house where he lived with his brother on first coming to America, which likewise is still extant? Why does he not haunt the cold shores of the Black Sea, where he laid low the Turks in the single fleet-command victory of his storied naval career? Why are there no records of him haunting the rooms on the Rue de Tournon in Paris where he met his illness-wracked demise at the age of forty-five? Or the Paris cemetery that was his home for more than a century? Modern buildings now stand above it, but no ponytailed, buckle-shoed gentleman wraith has been reported from this quarter.

No, for reasons we can only conjecture, the ghost of John Paul Jones has chosen to haunt only two places. One is where he rests for eternity, finally and with due honors after having his corpse suffer, first, ignominious anonymity, and then the disturbance of being shuffled about from place to place (surely such jostling could re-stir the deadest of the dead). And as for the other spot, might his haunting presence be (Jones was, after all, a rather legendary ladies' man) for the love of a woman?

The colorful details of his life, his rise from modest beginnings to grand influencer of events in his earth-altering era, are well known: how he was born a gardener's son on the banks of Solway Firth in 1747. How he went to sea at the age of thirteen. How, on a trading voyage during which the captain and chief mate perished of fever, young John took charge with coolness and success, and thus rose to his first command while only twenty-one. How on a later voyage he killed a mutineer in self-defense. How he was convinced to flee to the American colonies, where he abandoned his birth name, John Paul, for the alias Paul Jones, and later, finally, became John Paul Jones.

His adventurous life course swept him into the swirling political maelstroms of his century, and he relished the tumult. He later would voice a sentiment, popular among the Enlightenment thinkers of the time, that he liked to fancy himself a citizen of the world. The mystic cabalism of Freemasonry appealed to him early on; he petitioned for, and received, admission into St. Bernard's Lodge, Kilwinning Number 122, of the Ancient Society of Free and Accepted Masons in 1770. His entry into this mysterious brotherhood would have profound impacts throughout his life. It was Masonic associations that paved the way for Jones' entry as an officer into the fledgling Continental Navy in 1775. A few years hence, once he had become the swashbuckling hero of the seas and the toast of France, he was admitted into the exclusive, powerful Lodge of the Nine Sisters—

Europe's most influential and important Masonic order—whose members included such luminaries as Benjamin Franklin and Voltaire. Jones was now party to weird, clandestine ritualism in the Jesuit grounds on the Rue de Pot de Fer Sainte-Sulpice, where he was hailed by his confreres as the very scion of the ancient gods of war and wisdom.

But all that was still in the future when he set forth on a path for glory in the opening year of the American Revolution. He received his lieutenant's commission in December 1775; by 1777 he had his own command, the *Ranger*. Jones took up lodgings in Portsmouth, New Hampshire, while the *Ranger* was being built there and was quite taken with the town. He later would write that the happiest days of his life were in Paris and Portsmouth. Jones not only loved Portsmouth, he loved certain of its ladies as well, and they loved him in return.

Jones sailed in command of the *Ranger* until 1779, when he became the proud recipient of a gift from the king of France—an old East Indiaman named the *Duc de Duras*. Jones overhauled the ship and redubbed her the *Bon Homme Richard* in homage to his patron Benjamin Franklin (a reference to Franklin's *Poor Richard's Almanack*). With the deck of the *Bon Homme Richard* rolling beneath his feet, Jones sailed into the history books.

In a bloody, tenacious, close-in fight, the *Bon Homme Richard* battled HMS *Serapis* off Flamborough Head in the North Sea on September 23, 1779. The engagement began poorly for Jones; the opening British broadside crippled the *Bon Homme Richard*, taking many of her guns and gunners out of the equation. Capt. Richard Pearson of the *Serapis* quite reasonably asked Jones if he was ready to surrender, eliciting Jones' immortal retort, "I have not yet begun to fight!" The American naval spirit was born that day in Jones' defiance and in the dogged, unyielding grit with which the *Bon Homme Richard*'s crew kept fiercely in the fray even while their ship was sinking beneath them and Royal Marine sharpshooters in the spars were decimating them from above. Jones lost his ship but won the battle—and undying fame.

Jones returned to Portsmouth, New Hampshire, in 1781 to oversee the construction of the *America*, which was to be the new nation's greatest ship, and his new command. While the ship was being built, Jones delved headlong again into the pleasures of the Portsmouth party circuit and romantic dalliances with the local ladies.

When Congress changed its mind, denied Jones his pending command, and instead offered the *America* as a gift to France, Jones swallowed his bile and roamed abroad. He was always a better captain than politician, and a role in the political and military affairs of the new United States of America was not in the cards. The circumstances under which the man who came to be regarded as the father of America's Navy ended up adrift in Europe after the Revolution are both ironic and sad. He did not, could not, give up the sea. He served for a time as a rear admiral in the imperial navy of Empress Catherine the Great of Russia. Finally defeated by illness, he died in Paris in 1792.

His gravesite was lost within the shifting topographies of that sprawling European capital, and it was not until 1905, after a six-year search, that American officials succeeded in unearthing the corpse of the Republic's first great naval hero. The cadaver's gruesome visage—desiccated, leather-like skin drawn taut over the skull; eye sockets hollow; hair now wildly long—provided an uncannily accurate match when overlaid with images of Jean-Antoine Houdon's anatomically precise bust of Jones. President Theodore Roosevelt had Jones' body escorted home by a squadron of four cruisers, which were joined by seven battleships for the ceremonial approach up the Chesapeake to a resting place worthy of the father of the Navy. His remains arrived at the U.S. Naval Academy in Annapolis on July 22, 1905. Congress had not yet appropriated funds for a proper tomb, so the corpse was stashed in a storage room in the basement of Bancroft Hall. After an official welcoming ceremony held on April 24, 1906, replete with a speech by President Roosevelt to a crowd of more than a thousand, Jones went back to the basement to await completion of his grand crypt beneath the Naval Academy chapel in 1913. Until he was laid to his final rest there, the body of John Paul Jones, still in limbo after having been recalled from more than a century's slumber, lay in the basement of Bancroft Hall.

He had known cozier quarters in his time. During his New Hampshire sojourns Jones had boarded at the Widow Purcell's house in Portsmouth, which today still stands as the John Paul Jones House Museum. The indications of Jones' ghostly presence there are generally attributed to the love affairs the lusty captain carried out at the premises. Next door to the Jones House is another historic edifice, the Rockingham Hotel, formerly the home of town patriarch Woodbury Langdon. A feminine specter dubbed "the White Lady of Rockingham" by resident poet and ghost witness Esther Buffler haunts this building. The ghost is possibly the wife of Woodbury Langdon—and a secret paramour of the rakish captain who was lodging just next door, according to the hushed and knowing gossip-lore that has been passed down in the seaport since colonial days.

If the lady ghost is still active, might that explain why the ghost of Jones has chosen to return here as well? Perhaps the two of them, in the afterlife, are continuing the torrid affair they once savored in the flesh. Paranormalists equipped with ghost-detecting divining rods have verified the captain's presence in Jones House. His chamber was one of the hotbeds of spectral signals. And indeed, a glowing white female ghost—none other than the White Lady of Rockingham herself, Mrs. Langdon—occasionally sneaks over from her usual haunts next door to tryst with Captain Jones. "Some say the vision of a lady with a pure ivory face has been seen peering from more than one window of the John Paul Jones house," Portsmouth historian Pamela Keene noted.

No one would deny a hard-fighting naval hero his onshore pleasures; both he and the lady clearly seem to be enjoying themselves. But Jones, ever the rover, has not entirely changed his wandering ways. He divides his manifestations between Portsmouth and his final (at last) resting place in Annapolis, his southern headquarters for rampant ghostly activity.

Creepy noises emanate from his crypt at night. Over the years, honor guards have reported ghostly sightings both visual and auditory. Jones has been spotted standing among the marbled columns of the crypt, and a garbled, unsettling voice—a voice muffled and indistinct yet insistent—has been heard on numerous occasions. Indeed, one of the enduring legends ingrained in the lore of the Naval Academy tells of the honor guard who, driven insane by the manifestation of Captain Jones, was found leaning against the sarcophagus babbling in deranged conversation with the corpse entombed within.

Another guard engaged in a dialogue with the captain's ghost only with great reluctance. The crypt was devoid of visitors one afternoon when the guard was assailed from behind by a commanding basso profundo voice: "What . . . is . . . your name, sailor?"

The guard stared straight ahead with all the sentinel sangfroid he could muster.

The silence was broken again: "What . . . is . . . your name, sailor?"

This time, he turned.

The ghost was close, iridescent, bedecked in the garb of a bygone century.

The guard fought the panic inundating his veins.

The ghost smiled now, staring him in the face, and once again asked, "What ... is ... your name, sailor?"

The guard did the only thing he could think to do: he answered.

John Paul Jones nodded slowly, then pivoted and loped out of the crypt.

The guard, now beyond panic and into the realm of stunned disorientation, quickly followed.

The sun was bright, and John Paul Jones was gone.

Odds are he had a lady friend up north who was just dying to see him.

Spirits in the Timbers

S he won the young Republic's first major sea victory, fought the slave trade, and saw service in two world wars. She survived the conflagrations of battle and the ravages of time. She has been rebuilt repeatedly and debated over endlessly. "Huzzah for the *Constellation!*" rang the refrain of America's first triumphal sea ballad. Of the fledgling U.S. Navy's original six frigates, she was the first successfully launched down the slipway. Reborn in the mid-nineteenth century as a sloop-of-war, she was the last pure exemplar of the American age of fighting sail. Long is her lineage; much has she seen; many are the generations who manned her; and numerous are the sailor souls who remain aboard her for eternity. Indeed, the grand old USS *Constellation* is reputed to be "one of the most haunted sites in America."

The Continental Navy left a legacy of glory but no legacy of ships. The last vessel that had sailed forth in the cause for independence met her end in the wrecker's yard in 1785. But the infant nation soon felt the sting of John Paul Jones' prophetic words: "Alas, for the nation without a Navy." The Barbary pirates were wreaking havoc on American merchant ships in the Mediterranean—plundering them, imprisoning their crews, and exacting steep ransoms from the cash-strapped, still-faltering new United States of America. Thus did Congress in 1794 authorize the construction of a naval fleet to protect American citizens and American interests on the world's oceanic trade routes. In six American seaports, plans were laid out and timber was gathered for the first six vessels of the United States Navy.

The ships would be commanded by sea-wise veteran officers from the Revolution, and each ship's construction was overseen by the captain who would eventually command her. The frigate taking shape in David Stodder's shipyard in Baltimore, Maryland, was assigned to Thomas Truxtun, who had sailed the seas as a privateer in the Revolutionary War. Rotund, florid-faced, a stern taskmaster, and a tough captain to serve under, Truxtun was demanding and often ill-tempered, but he was brilliant and bold as well. The completed craft launched with great fanfare before a massed crowd at Baltimore on September 7, 1797, was a beauty to behold. She was beautiful in the way that great sailing ships are beautiful—neither frivolous nor luxurious, but impeccably functional. She was 171 feet long, weighed 1,265 tons, was armed with 36 guns, and sported a mainmast towering 150 feet above the deck. She was the *Constellation*, named for that newest constellation in the firmament of nations, that assemblage of stars on the blue field of the U.S. flag. She was a frigate—smaller than a ship of the line but still brimming with firepower, and swift and maneuverable to boot. She slipped into the water that first day with perfect grace.

She would test her mettle not against the Barbary corsairs, for that problem had temporarily abated while other trouble was brewing at sea— French trouble. America's erstwhile ally, livid over American trade with Britain and plundering ever-increasing amounts of American merchant shipping in revenge, became the Republic's first naval foe. It was an undeclared war, but it was war nonetheless.

The *Constellation* was off the coast of Nevis on February 9, 1799, when she sighted a large ship, evidently a ship-of-war, standing to westward. Truxtun ordered the British signal colors run up; the mystery ship responded suspiciously. Truxtun then ordered the American signals up; the other ship clearly did not know the flag code. Truxtun ordered battle stations and full sail on. Cannon muzzles emerged, and the *Constellation's* hull now bristled with deadly projectile force. Cutlasses and pistols were issued. Sailors scampered like monkeys into the vast forest of canvas and rigging. Lieutenants stood by their gun crews, ready for the bloody work to come. The American frigate flew across the waves, and the mystery ship revealed herself with a signal shot to windward and the raising of her true colors at last: the French tricolor.

The French craft made a run for it with the *Constellation* in hot pursuit. The American was gaining distance, but then, call it what you will—a singular random meteorological circumstance or the hand of national destiny—a vicious squall arose and the Caribbean Sea turned into a churning cauldron of angry waves beneath an afternoon sky gone suddenly black. As the wind howled and the tropical rains pummeled the rolling decks, the two ships enmeshed in their game of chase seemed suddenly diminutive, toys teetering on the edge of the abyss. Some back home had thought the

Constellation too top-heavy with sail, and that her speed would come at the sacrifice of stability. Here was a test. Truxtun, his old privateer's hunting instincts fully roused, was determined to run down his French quarry, squall be damned. As the *Constellation* lurched and leaned over the peaks and valleys of storm waves, he ordered just enough sails reefed to keep her from toppling without abandoning the pursuit. Fortune would prove to be on his side. The French ship's main topmast came crashing down amid the raging elements, slowing her fatally. And then, as quickly as it had arisen, the squall passed.

The *Constellation* thus won the chase and closed in on the French warship's lee quarter. She proved to be *L'Insurgente*. Hails arose from the cornered foe as the *Constellation* approached; Truxtun stood on the quarterdeck, coolly silent as the *Constellation* eased into point-blank range. French gunners stood at the ready, staring across at their American counterparts. Now that he had been outrun, the French captain was babbling for a parley. Truxtun's answer was terse and unequivocating: "Fire!" And down the rows of gun crews the word echoed, from officer to officer. With a horrible roar the *Constellation*'s guns erupted, pounding the enemy hull with a ferocious barrage of 24-pound double-loaded cannon fire. The French frigate immediately replied to the broadside in kind, and for more than an hour the ships traded fierce cannonades, the air dense with smoke-stench and flying splinters, with shouts of command and screams of the bloodied and the dying.

The French fought with a certain fastidiousness born of avarice. Hoping to secure a valuable prize, they aimed at the *Constellation*'s masts in order to disable her but not inflict a death blow. The Americans fought British style: brutally bludgeon the foe's hull; pound him into submission with unchecked violence; worry about winning the fight first and to the devil with the condition of the prize afterward. The *Constellation* struck her deadliest blow with a wicked circling maneuver that took her across the bow of the French frigate. Each of the *Constellation*'s 24-pounders in turned fired straight down the length of the enemy's deck, ripping materiel and men to shreds. Continuing to circle, the *Constellation* pounded out another broadside, then came around across *L'Insurgente*'s stern and unleashed yet another staccato sequence of merciless deck-length cannon fire. Three times the *Constellation* raked the French vessel fore and aft, until her deck was crimson with Gallic blood. Lt. John Rogers, commanding a *Constellation* gun crew, reported, "Although I would not have you think me bloody minded, yet I must confess the most gratifying sight my eyes ever beheld was seventy French pirates (you know I have just cause to call them such) wallowing in their gore."

In the heat and din of the fight, a young American seaman named Neal Harvey felt the cold, raw panic that only someone who has experienced close-in bloodshed can know. In his terror, Harvey lost all composure and suddenly fled from his station. Lt. Andrew Sterrett, in command of the gun crew on which Harvey served, exploded with rage. As the battle swirled around them, he chased Harvey down, cornered him, and impaled him on cold steel. "One fellow I was obliged to run through the body with my sword, and so put an end to a *coward*," Sterrett boasted afterward. "You must not think this strange, for we would put a man to death for even looking pale on board *this* ship."

And so the official report of the first major sea victory by an American-made warship included a haunting and terse entry on the casualty list: "Neal Harvey, killed for cowardice."

The *Constellation* compounded her initial success by battling the frigate *La Vengeance* in February 1800 in a bloody, five-hour night fight from which the young U.S. Navy emerged victorious again. The French now had a nickname for the *Constellation;* they called her "the Yankee Racehorse."

The Racehorse went on to fight in the Barbary Wars, but in the War of 1812 she was sidelined into a largely defensive role by the British blockade. She chased slavers in the 1820s and circumnavigated the globe in the 1840s. And periodically she was brought into port and rebuilt. After the 1853 rebuilding at the Gosport Navy Yard, the *Constellation* emerged as essentially a new ship—a sloop-of-war now rather than a frigate. That final rebuilding started a rancorous debate among naval architecture historians that rages to this day. Was she still the same ship?

For years, conventional wisdom held that the 1797 frigate and the 1854 sloop-of-war were indeed the same *Constellation*, drastically altered yet with a continuum of identity. But the conventional wisdom shifted in the late twentieth century, and with it the official Navy line, which now treats the original frigate *Constellation* and the sloop-of-war *Constellation* as two distinct vessels.

But the issue is not so simply resolved. Great minds have grappled with the concept of identity continuity ever since Plato ruminated about Heraclitus' river and Plutarch pondered the paradox of the Ship of Theseus. Modern philosophy, through the intertwining skeins of physical continuity theory, personal identity theory, and (most germane to a ship debate) spatio-temporal continuity theory, actually supports the one-ship contention. To wit: an object—be it a ship undergoing multiple increasingly elaborate rebuilds, a tadpole metamorphosing into a frog, or a person growing through continuous and complete molecular changeovers from infant to adult—maintains its core selfhood even as its components alter through the years, as long as it adheres to a traceable identity course through time and space. In short, "A and B can truly be said to have the same body, even though the body at the later time has no matter in common with the body at the earlier time."

In the *Constellation*'s case, that last point is actually moot. There *is* some remnant matter from the original vessel in the rebuilt ship. The *Constellation* Museum in Baltimore acknowledges this crucial detail. When the *Constellation* was refurbished as the 1854 sloop-of-war, "eight pieces of the original ship [were] included in her construction," thereby establishing "a provenance dating back to the Baltimore-built U.S. Frigate *Constellation* of 1797."

All other arguments aside, there is salient proof that the *Constellation* of today has in her bones the *Constellation* of 1797—and that is the persistent presence of pre-1854 ghosts that haunt her decks. "Whatever was left of the original vessel," a paranormal investigator reported, "its use in the new ship was enough to keep the ghosts around."

And others soon joined them. John Campbell, Captain of the Forecastle on the new sloop-of-war, went overboard on March 16, 1862, and rescue efforts failed to retrieve him. By that fall, his waterlogged ghost was being observed alongside the lee cathead. In June 1863 another sailor who had died recently began reappearing, singing. By the 1870s, the ship's log was recording orders to crew members "to stop saluting ghosts."

Saluted or not, the ghosts of the *Constellation* grew to be protective of her as she advanced in age. In 1926, while she was at the Philadelphia Naval Shipyard, a fire broke out amidships. Miraculously, the blaze seemed to have extinguished itself by the time firemen arrived on the scene. The old wooden craft should have gone up like a box of matches. The incident remains a mystery.

Diverse odd occurrences haunted the old vessel while she lay moldering at the Newport, Rhode Island, Navy Yard: Navy men disrupted and disturbed by strange voices and fleeting figures, the stalking shadows of multiple generations of seafaring fighters, the jangled echoes of long years of service on many seas. The bloodied, ancient decks creaked beneath history's footsteps, and the sailor dead still laid claim to their billets and made their lingering presence known.

During World War II, President Franklin D. Roosevelt resurrected the storied *Constellation,* appointing her the Flagship of the Atlantic Fleet and thereby recruiting the ghostly heroes of old to lend their spiritual hands to the cataclysmic struggle. Did their otherworldly intervention help turn the tide of war? FDR's summoning of said spirits may not have been entirely inadvertent; he was known to be intrigued by occult possibilities and fascinated with spiritualism, a trait inherited from the Delano side of his family. After the war, the ship was moved to Boston Harbor to wallow alongside her younger sister, the *Constitution.* And there she sat, the once mighty *Constellation,* descending further and further into barnacled, splintering decay. In 1953 a group of Baltimoreans raised the money to bring the *Constellation* home to her birth port for long-overdue restoration. And in 1955, with great fanfare and national celebration, the *Constellation* came home to Baltimore. As workmen got busy on the Herculean task of restoring the historic vessel, they soon realized that they were not the only ones on board.

"Whatever it was—the phosphorescently glowing, translucent ectoplasmic manifestation of a late Eighteenth Century or an early Nineteenth Century United States Navy captain, or something else—it strode across the quarterdeck of the United States Frigate *Constellation* at Fort McHenry Thursday night," the *Baltimore Sun* reported on December 31, 1955.

The sighting was captured on camera by Lt. Cdr. Allen Ross Brougham, USNR, who had heard the disturbing accounts that started when the rotting hull first arrived in Baltimore Harbor from Boston the previous September. "Firemen said they heard strange noises and saw strange shapes aboard," noted Brougham. Furthermore, "when she was moved to the dock across from the USS *Pike,* crewmen on gangway watch on the submarine reported the same phenomena—strange shapes, strange noises."

Skeptical at first, Brougham grew intrigued by the strange stories emanating from the decrepit old vessel whose weathered planks were steeped in history and blood. He consulted a psychic researcher, who informed him that "the best time to observe apparitions of this nature is at midnight during the period between Christmas and the new year." They set up a camera rig that scoped the quarterdeck, and almost precisely at midnight—11:59 and 47 seconds, to be exact—a ghost made his shocking, albeit brief, appearance.

Brougham snapped the picture, all the time in a state of awed disbelief. "How can one describe a ghost?" he later reflected. "It'd be difficult to do it justice—the sudden, brightening blueish-white radiance; the translucency."

The creepy photograph, published in the *Sun*, showed a blurred humanoid shape between the deck rail and the ship's wheel. The spectral figure appeared to be moving forward purposefully. "I was aware somehow that he was motivated by a sense of great urgency," Brougham recalled. Certain visual aspects were suggestive of military attire. "Our subject was wearing a definitely dated uniform. I'm no expert on early navy uniforms. But the gold-striped trousers, the cocked hat, the heavy gold epaulets, the sword—or what appeared to be these—looked to me like the sort of uniform that might have been worn by an officer around the year 1800. And it—or he—was—or seemed to be—a captain."

A diagonal swath of fuzzed darkness seemed to indicate an arm reaching across the midsection. "He was reaching across his waist with his right hand, as though just about to draw his sword."

That Brougham managed to capture the image is fortuitous, for there was scant opportunity to do so, particularly in his stunned state. "It was all over within the time he took to make a single stride."

In the ensuing years, workmen enacting the *Constellation*'s repairs were shaken by weird, plaintive moans and baleful cries emanating from belowdecks. In every case, when they sought the source of the voices, silence greeted them in the dim recesses below. A human—or humanoid shape—was spotted lurking on the gun deck one summer evening; no visitors were allowed aboard at that hour, so the police were summoned. The officers brought with them a police dog, a redoubtable German shepherd whose sharply honed ferocity was enough to cow the boldest criminal. The dog's handler ordered him to advance into the bowels of the ship and corner the trespasser—but the dog's impeccable training failed him, as did his normal courage. There he stood, impervious to his orders—incapable of obeying them—quaking spasmodically in terror, neck hairs standing at porcupine attention. He simply would not go another step farther. The frightened lawmen reluctantly went below in the dog's stead, and discovered . . . nobody.

And there was the occasion when a group of visitors witnessed the panic-inducing spectacle of the ship's wheel being turned—rapidly, repeatedly, and determinedly—hard to starboard by the unseen hands of an invisible helmsman. "Nonsense!" the skeptic retorts. "Wind was pushing the rudder, in turn spinning the wheel." Not in this case. The cable connecting the wheel and rudder was not attached; nothing natural made that heavy old wheel turn. Logic's finger must point inexorably, with dread, to a supernatural mover.

A more visible manifestation appeared to a girl on board for a youth-group Halloween dance. Resting between numbers on a bulkhead bench, she turned her head to talk to her date—but no young man was sitting next to her. It was an ancient mariner, close up and face to face, and he was smiling at her. Before she could gather her thoughts, the strange sailor vanished. The girl, unaware of the stories of *Constellation* hauntings, assumed it was some old salt who was on the ship for one reason or another. But no such living individual was supposed to be there that evening, and the young lady's description of the wizened sailor matched that of an entity in an earlier unexplained encounter—with a Catholic priest.

The previous run-in had transpired in July 1959. The *Constellation*, open to the public while repairs were under way, was still in a sorry state but had already become a magnet for the historically curious. The priest, on an East Coast sojourn from his home parish in Detroit, asked permission to come aboard early that summer morning. Visitors' hours did not commence until 10 AM, but the priest had an 11 AM berth on the Washington-bound train. Donald Stewart, the *Constellation*'s curator, consented but made it clear that he was too busy to provide a guided tour. The priest, grateful enough for the rule bending that allowed him up the gangplank, headed off on his own to explore.

Later, when the priest resurfaced abovedecks, beaming after his inspection of the ship, Stewart apologized again for not having been able to be of service as a guide.

The priest said that it was quite all right; he had enjoyed a wonderful tour courtesy of "the old gent."

The incredulous curator said, "What old gent?"

The priest described the kindly elderly man in sailor's garb who had offered him the full docent treatment, leading the way and pointing out various details of interest. "He showed me all around and was very nice," the priest said.

"Ridiculous!" the curator responded. "Let's have a look below."

The pair searched the ship thoroughly, but there was no one else on board. The priest's cheerfulness had left him now, replaced by the damp grip of terror. Suddenly eager to leave the *Constellation*, he clambered ashore with all deliberate speed.

Was the grinning old sailor encountered by the teenager and the priest the same ghost spotted by watchman Carl Hansen one night while Carl was playing cards? Looking up from his hand, Hansen stared in mute awe as an aged figure in naval uniform appeared out of nowhere, hovered, then walked right through the bulkhead, disappearing into the wood.

By the mid-1960s such incidents had become so shockingly recurrent that the *Constellation* committee deemed it necessary to recruit the services of paranormalist professionals. A request letter went out to Hans Holzer, one of the world's top ghost investigators and a prolific occult-book author of international renown. Holzer arrived in Baltimore on a stormy October evening in 1966. He rendezvoused with the clairvoyant witch Sybil Leek, twentieth-century Britain's greatest psychic, and went aboard the ship. As soon as they were on the main deck, Leek became distraught. Without benefit of lighting, she hastily began to make her way through the blackness to the haunted ship's aural nerve centers. The rest of the party caught up with her at the after orlop deck, where she came to a sudden stop, shivering and upset, and said, "There is much evil here."

Like a human divining rod to the world beyond, she had zeroed in on "a presence, lots of atmosphere . . . very cruel." At first she thought it was a baby that she heard crying. Then, as the psychic signals came more clearly, she realized it was an eleven-year-old boy—being murdered.

Constellation authorities accompanying the investigation felt themselves in the maw of horror when they realized that they were standing right where the surgeon's quarters had been; and in olden days naval surgeons employed cabin boys as assistants. As she stood there channeling the tragedy, Leek was ascertaining before their very eyes that just such a surgeon's boy had been slain here by a pair of crewmen in August 1822.

Probing further into the ship's recesses, Leek came into contact with other ghostly occupants—two men, it seemed: one named something like "Thraxton" (most likely Captain Truxtun, of whom the British clairvoyant had never heard), and the other a more vague, more enigmatic presence. The latter turned out to be two others. Leek thought she was psychically receiving a name that sounded like "Harsen." Great sadness accompanied some of the vibrations, paradoxically alternating with a sense of profound happiness.

Finally, she was able to sort through the garbled transmissions from the netherworld to glean both the morose presence of Neal Harvey, whose execution for cowardice in 1799 had fated him to walk these decks for eternity, and the contented presence of a much newer resident, none other than Carl Hansen, the *Constellation*'s night watchman from 1958 to 1963. After being replaced by a burglar alarm, old Hansen lobbied constantly to get his job back, but to no avail. He had wanted more than anything to be on board the *Constellation* again. And he had just recently died.

Saved from the withering decay of time and tide, the newly restored *Constellation* took her place at Baltimore's *Constellation* Dock in 1972 and quickly became a popular destination for visitors to the city. Many were interested in no more than the ship's martial history, but the Holzer-Leek investigation had become a cause-célèbre in occult science circles, turning the haunted ship into a pilgrimage point for people who, either for purposes of serious research or for the thrilling intoxicant of a brief brush with the lingering dead, were delving into such matters in ever-expanding ranks in the 1960s and 1970s.

An artist, a college professor, a high school teacher, a psychology student, numerous married couples, and "an elderly woman who wanted to bring her own medium along" were among the fifty or so specter-seekers who in November 1970 formally applied to the *Constellation* restoration committee for permission to hold an all-night séance aboard the ghost-laden vessel. While committee chairman Gordon M. F. Stick found the request worthy of interest, and even considered joining the experiment himself, the rest of the committee did not share his stance. After weeks of deliberation they voted overwhelmingly against granting such access. Holzer and Leek had been invited and accompanied by *Constellation* officials, but fifty paranormal experimenters on board overnight was deemed too phantasmagoric a scenario for the floating shrine. Noting that "the Navy might also look askance at such an event," Stick conceded to his committee's vote. "Personally," he commented, "I have an open mind on psychic phenomena. At the same time I must ignore my own feelings and go along with the majority." A local businessman who had been among the séance-requesting horde refused to accept the rejection: "As far as I'm concerned, this is not the end of the matter. And I think others will feel as I do."

He was right. In subsequent years the ship's controlling body would prove more receptive to ghost investigators eager to explore the apparitional hotspot. One group of visitors had a familial connection to the ship's ranking spirit. Some two hundred descendants of Thomas Truxtun, converging from eighteen states and ranging in age from infants to elders, gathered at the *Constellation* for a family reunion in 1976. Having heard the accounts of their ancestor's spectral presence, the clan anticipated some sort of manifestation. The old salt didn't disappoint. As two of the descendants stood alongside the empty ship at midnight, one of them said, "Hurry up and do something, Commodore. It's late and I want to go to bed!" In immediate reply, "a deafening slap in the water thundered immediately in front of us . . . wooden fenders rocked wildly between ship and pier, splashing water. . . . Like Abbott and Costello, we leapt three feet in the air and grabbed at one another."

Paranormal research technology became increasingly refined in the years that followed, and the *Constellation* continued to offer opportunities for its application. In the early years of the new millennium the *Constellation* was undergoing state-of-the-art scrutiny by wireless video, infrared cameras, digital thermometers, and electromagnetic field detectors. She continued to attract local paranormal organizations, Canadian TV documentarians, and sundry other spirit-seekers from points in between.

At century's end, due for repairs and subject to architectural reinterpretation, the *Constellation* was given an overhaul, and in 1999 she was unveiled anew, now reconfigured along her 1854 sloop-of-war lines. To the passerby not immersed in the arcane minutiae of nautical construction, she remained as she had been before—a beautiful old floating relic from the age of sail, wonderfully incongruous amid the surrounding modernity. She had long since established herself as the visual and spiritual epicenter of the bustling, congested, horn-honking cityscape surrounding her. In the early twenty-first century an estimated 100,000 visitors were boarding her every year.

And the ghostly sightings continued apace: faces in the gun ports, leering in the night; footfalls tramping on empty decks; Christmas tree lights tampered with in the office when no one was there to do it; the tinny melody of a long-ago cease-fire bugle; an unidentified sailor ambling about the gun deck wearing a look of deep sorrow; sounds and movements of some unseen crew rushing about in a great hurry. In many cases, the smell of gunpowder presaged a ghost's appearance. A *Constellation* staffer inspecting the orlop deck with a flashlight witnessed the sudden appearance of an amorphous white fog. The evanescence congealed into humanoid form—a humanoid in archaic sailor's garb—and approached the staffer, who remained frozen with fear as the apparition walked right through him.

The staffer might have been alone down in that dark hold, but the ghostly sailor was not. The *Constellation* is teeming with his shipmates, with souls that have seeped into the timbers. Some, like old Truxtun, are there by choice, reliving past glories. Others, like sad Harvey, are there by fate, bound to the decks that absorbed their blood amid roar of cannon and clash of steel.

The Flaming Ghost Ship
of Mahone Bay

Some vessels enter the eternal ghost fleet by succumbing to the cruel and fickle elements. Some go there fighting, bested in battle and consigned to the depths. Some, perhaps the most tragic of all, die of self-inflicted wounds.

Such was the fate of the *Young Teazer*, a swift and successful privateer in life, a floating conflagration thereafter. Like her sister phantom the *Dash*, the *Young Teazer* was a proud component of the quasi-navy that buttressed the fledgling U.S. Navy in the War of 1812: predatory vessels legitimized by letters of marque roving forth as sea rogues for the Republic. Devils by Divine Providence, one might ironically observe. Intrepid, opportunistic, combining Yankee sea-craft with high-risk stratagem, these raiders cockily coauthored the American naval story in those dire days when a new nation's tentative existence hung in the balance. "The history of the United States Navy is so intimately connected with that of our privateers," noted the historian Edgar Stanton Maclay, "that the story of one would be incomplete without a full record of the other."

In her brief, rash career, the *Young Teazer* wreaked havoc and then died shockingly. Her gory finale, however, was merely her new beginning. Generations have arisen and rotted away since her wartime exploits, and yet she lives on, a recurrent sea specter whose name is spoken in hushed voices when the fog rolls in along the Nova Scotia coast.

She was a sleek two-masted schooner, 124 tons burthen, 75 feet long, copper-hulled, bedecked with five guns. A carved alligator head, jaws opened to strike, adorned her bow. Speed was her weapon, and oarsmen on sixteen sweeps augmented her sail power when the wind grew light. As her name suggested, *Young Teazer* had a predecessor—*Teazer* by name, owned by the same New York concern and a rapacious privateer in her own right

during the first year of the War of 1812. The first *Teazer* had garnered her
share of prize captures and enjoyed her share of tight scrapes and close
escapes before finally coming to an outlaw end, captured and torched by
HMS *San Domingo* in December 1812.

The first *Teazer's* crew members were hauled to Halifax, Nova Scotia,
as prisoners of war. Her captain, Frederick Johnson, was granted the
parole privilege generally afforded to officers and gentlemen. By affixing
his scrawl to the requisite papers Johnson gained a modicum of personal
freedom—but at the price of swearing never again to set sail in hostile
fashion against the interests of His Majesty. It was a courtesy between
gentlemen—a courtesy underscored by the threat of the hangman's rope if
the pledge were broken.

By all accounts Johnson was a nasty man, foul-tempered and disliked.
A prisoner exchange soon found him back on American soil, where the
temptation of further privateering exploits and profits quickly led him
to break his parole pledge. Some token credit might seem due to one in
whom the pull of high-seas adventure was so strong, but Johnson's subsequent actions would prove so irredeemably heinous as to preclude for all
time any generosity of spirit toward him.

Fresh from the original *Teazer*, Johnson signed on as first lieutenant
of the *Young Teazer*. The newly built privateer was readying for her maiden
voyage under audacious Capt. W. B. Dobson, whom one historian labeled
"an ideal privateersman." She put out of New York on May 10, 1813. On
the thirteenth she spied her first promising-looking prize, a sizable black
two-topsail schooner. The chase lasted five hours. In range at last, the
Young Teazer opened fire, hurling twenty-one shots from her 12-pounders
and fifteen shots from her 9-pounders. The schooner kept running, but
the Americans knew they had wounded her and laid on sail to continue
the pursuit. As they came up on her again, their quarry hove around to
greet them warmly this time. Broadsides erupted in exchange, and smoke
filled the space between the rival craft. The *Young Teazer* unleashed another
broadside, and when the smoke cleared, Dobson and the crew could see
that their prey had struck her colors. Just three days out from port, and the
raider had wrested her first capture.

And a worthy capture she was: the *Invincible Napoleon*, a French six-
teen-gunner with a hundred-man crew. The prize's topsy-turvy history
reflected the maritime tenor of the times: originally launched as a French
privateer, the *Invincible Napoleon* had changed hands constantly, first being

captured by the British brig-of-war HMS *Native*, then captured by the Yankee privateer *Alexander*, then captured by the British frigates HMS *Shannon* and *Tenedos*. Now she was back in American hands, soon to draw a tidy sum on the auction block at Portland, Maine.

The French schooner was not the only capture netted during the *Young Teazer*'s inaugural run; on May 24 the privateer traded cannon fire with HMS *Ann* and bested that brig as well. Here was another prize that had flown beneath alternating flags: British, then American, then British again until falling into the *Young Teazer*'s clutches. She, too, was bound for the Portland auctioneer. Interestingly, her last British recapture had been by HMS *La Hogue*, a seventy-four-gun ship of the line that was to play a crucial role in the fate of the *Young Teazer*.

After adding a schooner to her list of captures, the *Young Teazer* returned to port to celebrate her successful first voyage. Flush with her initial victories and brimming with confidence, with bold Dobson at the helm, she set forth anew in June 1813—never to return.

The brig *Sir John Sherbrooke*, an aggressive and powerful Nova Scotian privateer (whose original incarnation had been as the American brig-of-war USS *Rattlesnake*), was a 273-ton eighteen-gunner with a 150-man crew. She caught the *Young Teazer* at the mouth of Halifax Harbor and gave chase. With the brig cutting off the seaward route, Dobson improvised craftily. He ordered the British colors hoisted and quickly assumed the role of a British prize master bringing his captured American schooner into port. He sailed into heavily fortified Halifax Harbor as if he owned it. The suspicious *Sir John Sherbrooke* followed until the American privateer was under the guns of the British fort. When the land troops bought the deception and the shore guns did not fire on the apparent prize vessel, the *Sir John Sherbrooke* was convinced as well and stood back out to sea. Captain Dobson waited until nightfall, then scooted off with all dispatch.

But Dobson's brazenness knew no bounds. Having parlayed an outlandish bluff into a hair's-breadth escape, he now sent a proclamation landward "declaring all Halifax in a state of blockade." It was, a contemporary noted, a "piece of audacious impudence," and one instantly compounded. Knowing that HMS *La Hogue*, the mighty seventy-four-gunner whose destiny had been hovering at the periphery of the *Young Teazer*'s, was the dominant Royal Navy ship in these waters, Dobson also sent ashore a challenge to her, boasting he would fight the larger ship "at any time and place." The *La Hogue* got word and accepted the gauntlet slap—much more quickly than Dobson had anticipated. The British giant hove into view seemingly out of the blue, and the *Young Teazer* was in for the run of her short life.

The frigates *Orpheus* and *Castor* and the brig-of-war *Manly* soon joined the pursuit, with the *La Hogue* at the head of the pack. The *Young Teazer* dashed back into Halifax Harbor, but the fort's gunners would not be fooled again; the privateer found herself with land cannon to the lee and ships' cannon to seaward. For eighteen long hours she skirted and dodged, finally running into Mahone Bay in search of waters too shoaly to allow the big ships to follow. From Sculpin Rock to Spindler's Cove, from Cross Island to Big Tancook, the privateer tacked and tacked, zigzagging away from the dogged ships of His Majesty King George III. As the sun went down on June 27, 1813, with the wind dead and overwhelmingly outnumbered, the *Young Teazer* had run out of tricks. The British had cornered her.

The shot of signal guns flew past, five Royal Navy cutters began lowering away, and 135 British sailors closed in for the capture. Captain Dobson summoned his officers for a consultation. All but one appeared. For as the British boats approached, there was an individual aboard the *Young Teazer* more chagrined than all the rest about their impending surrender and capture. Frederick Johnson, the volatile first officer, had far more to dread from John Bull's Navy than the others. Having violated his parole, he knew that a hastily strung yardarm noose awaited him. In a spasm of raw panic, Johnson grabbed a firebrand and charged toward the powder magazine. As Johnson dashed below, a horrified sailor bellowed a warning to the captain.

But Johnson was already in the magazine before anyone could move to stop him. As the Royal Navy boats drew ever closer, he introduced the torch to a barrel of gunpowder.

With an ear-shattering boom and a rushing roar, the *Young Teazer* exploded into flames. Burning timbers and burning, screaming men were flung through the air like fireballs as the inferno turned night into day. The blast was heard twelve miles away. Eight of the thirty-six-man crew survived, one without a leg, another with both feet blown off above the ankles. One of the survivors who had been sent flying from the deck managed to swim to the *Young Teazer*'s stern boat, cut it loose, and round up his few fellow survivors. They came ashore on Anshultz Island and turned themselves in. During his subsequent incarceration, one of those fortunate men said to a crewman from the *Sir John Sherbrooke*, "We saw you after us, and it would have been well if you had taken us."

The portion of the vessel that was not blasted into airborne splinters remained tenuously afloat, illuminating the night sky with towering, acrid flames. She had burned to the waterline by the time anyone could tow her ashore. The wood that was still salvageable—foremast and bowsprit of Norway pine, hull portions of American oak unscathed beneath copper skin—was sold for lumber. The salvaging process had been a gruesome undertaking, boats wending through the bloody debris that blanketed the sea surface. Some men fainted at the sight of the floating wreck, the headless and legless corpses, the sheer carnage.

It was the very sea of Hell, and it was all due to one Frederick Johnson. "Had Johnson blown his own brains out, or tied a gun about his neck, and thrown himself overboard, some would have mourned for him, and none found fault," a nineteenth-century chronicler remarked. "By all accounts he was not one of the most amiable men living; on the contrary, the desperate wretch must have been possessed of the devil, to have plunged so many human beings into eternity without a moment's warning. Many of them, it is said, had wives and children to mourn their untimely fate."

The townsfolk retrieved what charred and dismembered remains they could of the majority who had perished and interred them in the graveyard of St. John's Anglican Church. There still stands today a uniquely sad old cross of oak made from the *Young Teazer*'s timbers.

On June 27, 1814—one year to the day after the disaster—the fishing fleet was at work on Mahone Bay when a phantom vessel, engulfed in flames, emerged from the thick fog. As the apparition drew closer, fishermen gripped the rails in white-knuckle fear, for the burning craft was coming on too fast to evade. Then, as suddenly as she had appeared, the ghost ship vanished in a noisome eruption of smoke and fire. Witnesses on shore likewise looked on as the strange vision culminated explosively. And so it was that on the following year, the second anniversary of the *Young Teazer* tragedy, even more onlookers were gathered to see if the "fire ship" would reappear. She did. And she vanished in the same climactic fashion. A nineteenth-century Nova Scotian scribe recorded, "Resulting from these facts a superstition has arisen . . . that the *Teazer*, like the *Flying Dutchman* of old, supernaturally revisits the waters in which she met her fate."

And so began the legend of "the Teazer Light." Down through the long decades, countless horrified observers have witnessed the flaming ghost ship of Mahone Bay. Not every sighting has been bound strictly to the specific anniversary of the *Young Teazer*'s fiery demise, though that date remains the optimum time for a reappearance. The rustic fisherfolk of an earlier century have given way to such unimpeachable latter-day witnesses as an "average young couple" with a residential water view, a widely respected and highly regarded older couple, and a "well educated paramedic." Old salts eventually learned to glean portent from the burning vision; experience taught them that when the flaming ghost ship was sighted, a terrible storm was in the offing. Fishermen heeded the Teazer Light and stayed ashore. The light also came to be associated with the legendary Oak Island treasure, a hoard believed to be buried nearby that has been attributed to everyone from Captain Kidd to the Vikings to the Knights Templar. It is said that whenever someone gets close to finding the treasure, the Teazer Light blazes brightly in some weird occult affinity.

The numerous sightings have had their variances, but they have salient details in common: a vessel fully ablaze floating across the bay, a fearsome image that finally shocks the onlooker by culminating in a blinding explosion. The haunting often includes the wailing voices of the doomed, the insane screams of the burning in their death throes.

Pity the poor soul who, like those fishermen who first spied her, has the misfortune to be in a boat when the flaming ship bears down. Such a witness will be most susceptible to the sudden and irreversible whitening of the hair that derives from raw terror. Many have described the panicked feeling as the blazing phantom courses headlong toward them. Only in the final second before impact does the ghost ship burst into blinding light— and then she is gone.

But she will return. She must. Compelled by dark reasons beyond the boundaries of comprehension, she is doomed forever to relive that long-ago gruesome night when she was brought down by madness, treachery, and fire.

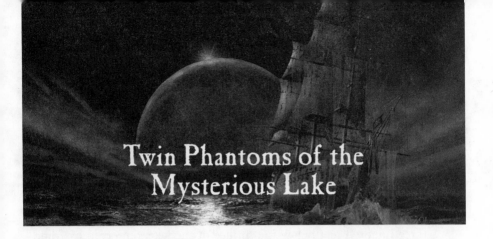

Twin Phantoms of the Mysterious Lake

To witness the appearance of a phantom ship is to scar one's psyche for life. Imagine, then, the impact of sighting *two* such ghostly vessels at once—a fate that has befallen many a stupefied mariner plying one of the most haunted bodies of water on Earth—Lake Ontario. This great inland sea is a notorious hotbed of anomalous occurrences, a nexus of the paranormal. Among its other disturbing distinctions, it is the final resting place of an inordinately high number of ships. Foremost among them are two U.S. Navy vessels that went down together in a freak squall and continue to reappear as floating wraiths, foul omens to any craft whose wake they happen to cross.

Procured during the massive Lake Ontario naval buildup in the War of 1812, sent to the cold depths with shocking suddenness and great loss of life, the *Hamilton* and *Scourge* linger like Gemini twins of sadness, two sets of luminescent sails moving mournfully across dark nocturnal waves. They sail at the vanguard of many oddities that bedevil this mysterious lake: strange disappearances, enigmatic power emanations, a superfluity of UFO sightings. Lake Ontario, for reasons researchers have yet to fathom, is a portal to the unknown.

The eastern portion of the lake is home to the infamous Marysburgh Vortex, sometimes popularly referred to as "the Great Lakes' Bermuda Triangle." Ships, aircraft, and individuals have vanished there without a trace. Monstrous creatures have been glimpsed. Bizarre electromagnetic phenomena have been detected, possibly in relation to the reported extraterrestrial encounters. Some scientists working on the fringes of their profession have even gone so far as to promulgate theories about invisible moving columns rising skyward from the lake in which the normal rules of time, space, and gravity do not apply. These pillars of molecular anarchy, which can generate severe atmospheric disturbances, are believed to emanate from variations in the Earth's magnetic field. (Lake Ontario is home to several well-documented magnetic anomalies, including the Sophiasburg Triangle.) Some think the columns "could be intermittently operational gateways to alternate dimensions." Most germane to our story, however, is that by shuffling the space-time deck and thereby warping reality, these traveling columns "explain the alleged mysterious floating ships and sailors' accounts of seeing ships that no longer existed."

Three hundred feet below the surface of the lake, preserved by frigid water, skeletons lie among cutlass and cannon in eternal repose on the *Hamilton* and *Scourge* shipwrecks. They are well west of the heart of the Marysburgh Vortex, itself an overpopulated ships' graveyard of wide renown. But the power of the Vortex reaches well beyond its parameters, generating unusual phenomena at least as far away as Lake Superior. Veteran Vortex researcher Hugh Cochrane described the "invisible cloak" spewed out by the Vortex that can "encompass and cause disasters in other parts of the Great Lakes, the regions surrounding them, and even the skies above. . . . [F]orces erupt with fury . . . releasing invisible and destructive energies."

It was just such a force erupting with just such fury that shook a glass-calm lake on the night of August 8, 1813, and destroyed two U.S. Navy schooners within minutes. If the invisible columns emanating from the Vortex help explain the prolific ghost ship sightings, then the "destructive energies" of the Vortex likewise can explain how a pair of ships became ghost ships in the first place.

But perhaps the Vortex was merely the catalyst for a doom foreordained. For as every superstitious sailor knows, it is bad luck to change the name of a vessel; and the *Hamilton* wasn't originally the *Hamilton*, and the *Scourge* wasn't originally the *Scourge*.

The *Hamilton* began existence as the merchant ship *Diana*, built at Oswego, on the New York side of Lake Ontario, in 1809. The Roman goddess for whom the craft was named graced the bowsprit as the figurehead. As war broke out anew between Great Britain and its erstwhile American colonies in 1812, the lake became crucial territory, lying at the fault line of the United States and British North America. Commo. Isaac Chauncey, actively beefing up the U.S. Navy presence on Lake Ontario, purchased the *Diana* from her original owner, the merchant Matthew McNair, in October 1812. The Navy renamed its new acquisition the *Hamilton* (in homage to Secretary of the Navy Paul Hamilton), and she joined the burgeoning fleet at Sacket's Harbor, New York. Anyone who happened to observe the figurehead of Diana as the ship was being renamed might have spied a frown on her face.

The *Scourge* originated as even more of an outlier. Built on the Canadian side and relinquished with vociferous objection, she had been christened, of all things, *Lord Nelson*, and Britain's greatest naval hero guided the merchant ship as the figurehead carving. She had been built at Niagara, Upper Canada, in 1811 and was the property of Canadian merchant James Crooks. On June 9, 1812 (before war was officially declared), the U.S. Navy cruiser *Oneida* intercepted the *Lord Nelson* and, citing the Embargo Act of 1807, confiscated her as a suspected smuggler. James Crooks launched an angry but futile protest that he maintained for the rest of his life. (His heirs finally realized some remuneration from the U.S. government in 1927.) The *Lord Nelson* was reborn as the *Scourge* and attached to the Sacket's Harbor armada. The name had been changed, but Admiral Nelson still gazed forth from his figurehead perch. It was as if Nelson himself had been pressed into service against the Royal Navy. Somewhere, the sea gods must have been furious.

Soon the two merchantmen's decks were straining beneath the weight of guns. The 73-foot, 76-ton *Hamilton* was refitted and armed with eight carronades—short-barreled 18-pounders good for close-in blasting—and a swiveling 32-pound cannon pivot-mounted amidships. The 57-foot, 45-ton *Scourge* now bristled with four 6-pound cannon and a quartet of 4-pounders to boot. Both schooners were ready for a fight, but both were perilously top-heavy now as well, brimming with war weight they had never been intended to bear.

"The day after I reached the harbour, I was ordered on board the *Scourge*," recalled Able Seaman Ned Myers, who recounted his memoirs to his old shipmate, the author James Fenimore Cooper. "This craft was unfit for her duty, but time pressed, and no better offered. . . . [S]he was so tender, that we could do little or nothing with her in a blow. It was often prognosticated that she would prove our coffin."

So be it; it was a dangerous time for all who served on Lake Ontario. The fate of the war on the northern frontier hung in the balance. The loss of naval footing on the vital water crossroads would be fatal to either side. So it was that a great arms race ensued between the British at their Kingston naval shipyard and the Americans at Sacket's Harbor forty miles to the south, which produced more U.S. Navy ships than any other American port during the War of 1812. It was a ceaseless game of martial one-upmanship that presaged the British-German battleship-building duel that preceded World War I, or the U.S.-Soviet nuclear arms contest of the Cold War. By the end of it, the British had floated onto Lake Ontario the mighty *St. Lawrence*, a 102-gun three-decker as large as any Royal Navy ship at the time. And the Americans had launched the *Superior*, the largest ship in the U.S. Navy. As these swelling rival fleets jockeyed for dominance, neither side dared risk annihilation. In adjacent Lake Erie, Commodore Chauncey's subordinate, Commo. Oliver Hazard Perry, would clash with the enemy in decisive fashion in September 1813, his valor and battle colors contributing to the Navy the undying words, "Don't give up the ship." But on Lake Ontario, high stakes and the shipbuilding race kept the situation in a Cold War–style standoff.

If Lake Ontario did not experience the naval Armageddon that the escalating warship tonnage threatened, it did see a good deal of fighting back and forth. The British raided Sacket's Harbor. The Americans raided Kingston and Fort George. Twice the Americans brought hell to York (modern-day Toronto). Both sides jabbed and parried, each waiting for the clear-cut opportunity to crush the other. And the *Hamilton* and *Scourge* did their part in these squadron maneuvers, citizen-schooners mustered into service and sallying forth as part of Chauncey's fleet.

Myers described the landing of troops off the *Scourge* during the April 1813 attack on York. "The English blazed away at us, concealed in a wood, and our men fired back again from the boat. . . . The shot flew pretty thick, and two of our oars were split." After landing the soldiers, Myers and the boat crew returned to the *Scourge* just as she was weighing anchor, joining the squadron moving in to fire on the York defenses. "We now had some sharp work with the batteries, keeping up a steady fire," Myers recounted. "We heard a magazine blow up, as we stood in, and this brought three cheers from us."

The Americans took the town and reveled in the streets. "I ought to feel ashamed, and do feel ashamed of what occurred that night," confessed Myers. He roved and raised hob with his gunnery crew, "five negroes, strapping fellows"; his merry band and the gun they manned were known fondly on board the *Scourge* as the Black Joke. "The recklessness of sailors may be seen in our conduct. All we received for our plunder was some eight or ten gallons of whiskey." By May, Myers and the Black Joke gang were back in the thick of it in the attack on Fort George: "We now kept up a steady fire with grape and canister, until the boats had got in-shore and were engaged with the enemy, when we threw round-shot, over the heads of our own men, upon the English." Once the American troops had been landed, "we sprung our broadside upon a two-gun battery that had been pretty busy, and we silenced that."

August came, and to their mutual astonishment the British and American squadrons found each other in sight proximity. Had there been breeze enough for battle that afternoon, an engagement surely would have ensued. As it was, the American squadron anchored on the listless surface of the lake and kept a wary eye on the nearby British. Sailors from the *Scourge* took one of the boats up the Black River to land a shooting party to kill game. They disembarked the huntsmen and then, coming back down-river, "saw something swimming, which proved to be a bear."

The firearms had gone ashore with the hunting party, so the boat crew grabbed anything at hand with which to beat back the bear. "We were an hour at work with this animal, the fellow coming very near mastering us," said Myers. "I struck at his nose with an iron tiller fifty times, but he warded the blow like a boxer . . . once or twice, he came near boarding us. At length a wood-boat gave us an axe, and with this we killed him."

A bear: an animal that loomed large in the indigenous mythologies of the northland and in the destinies of men. It was a nature spirit held in high esteem, and when one was slain, intricate atonement rites must be observed lest the elements be angered. "Indian hunters in the U.S.A. and Canada revere the creature," notes the definitive *Dictionary of Superstitions*, "and always give their apologies to any bear they have killed, laying out the different parts of its carcass according to ancient ritual."

It was to be the great misfortune of the sailors who killed the bear in this surreal encounter that they had no local shaman to consult. They are not to be blamed for battling and killing the monster, but perhaps pitied for their ignorance of the consequences. The bear's blood billowed into the water, and eldritch evils were aroused.

"Mr. Osgood had this bear skinned, and said he should send the skin to his family," said Myers. "If he did, it must have been one of the last memorials it ever got from him."

The British and American squadrons were still in sight of one another when the hunting party returned. A showdown seemed inevitable. But the water remained dead calm, and Chauncey chose to hover and wait for wind. "It was a lovely evening, not a cloud visible, and the lake being as smooth as a looking-glass," recalled Myers. "The English fleet was but a short distance . . . so near, indeed, that we could almost count their ports. They were becalmed, like ourselves, and a little scattered."

As the ships settled in for a tense nocturnal wait, the sails on the *Hamilton* and *Scourge* hung listless in the still air. The sails were left unfurled; there wasn't the least discernible breeze to threaten them. Though they bedded down, the crew remained ready for action as the sense of an impending beat-to-quarters hung heavy over their heads. "The captain looked at the heavens, and remarked that the night was so calm, there could be no great use in securing the guns," Myers said, "and the English were so near we should certainly engage, if there came a breeze."

Myers drifted to sleep on the glassy lake, then awoke "in consequence of large drops of rain falling on my face." He opened his eyes to a hellish maelstrom and a heaving deck. Loose cannon crushed men suddenly waking, screaming, and dying. "A flash of lightning almost blinded me. The thunder came at the next instant, and with it a rushing of winds that fairly smothered the clap."

The unfurled sail canvas ballooned and tore in the shrieking wind. "The instant I was aware there was a squall, I sprang for the jib-sheet," Myers recalled. He rallied help and cut rogue sails loose, a brave and futile gesture. "The water was now up to my breast, and I knew the schooner must go over." The world had turned topsy-turvy in "less than a minute."

Through the howls of nature and the howls of the dying Myers moved with the animal brain of survival. "The flashes of lightning were incessant, and nearly blinded me. . . . [T]he schooner was filled with the shrieks and cries of the men. . . . I now crawled aft . . . amid a most awful and infernal din of thunder . . . the wind blowing all the while like a tornado. . . . I made a spring . . . and fell into the water . . . the schooner sunk as I left her."

He swam furiously in the pitching swell of the lake surface gone mad. His thrown-forward hand landed on something solid: a boat torn asunder from the *Scourge*. "Had I swum another yard, I should have passed the boat, and missed her altogether!" Drowning would have been the inevitable consequence.

Myers climbed aboard and sought more survivors. "It rained as if the flood-gates of heaven were opened, and it lightened awfully. . . . My only chance of seeing was during the flashes . . . I could hear many around me, and, occasionally . . . in the flashes, I saw many heads, the men swimming in confusion, and at random." He rescued as many as the boat could hold. Some of the rescued were crewmen from another craft: the *Hamilton*. Soon it was clear that both had perished in the same blow, and with the same suddenness.

The little boat was filled, but the men it carried were a small fraction of the *Hamilton* and *Scourge* crews. Fifty-five men went down with the wrecks. Sixteen men survived. "These were all that were ever saved from the two schooners," Myers said. "The two commanders . . . were both lost. . . . All my Black Jokers were drowned. . . . The lake had swallowed up the rest of the two crews; and the *Scourge*, as had been predicted, had literally become a coffin to a large portion of her people."

Here in the thick of war came a horrific double sinking, a tragedy wrought not by the enemy but by capricious weather. It was the largest single loss of life on the Great Lakes during the War of 1812. The uncanny appearance of the squall that sank the *Hamilton* and *Scourge* astonished seasoned seamen at the time, and continues to be the stuff of speculation. Even the driest modern-day list of shipwrecks will categorize it as "a very unusual storm." Those who study the paranormal will go even further and say what was already on the minds of many: that the storm was an anomaly—that it was the work of the Marysburgh Vortex.

Records of the time and from even further back into at least the eighteenth century are rife with descriptions of inexplicable phenomena on Lake Ontario. Ojibway legends spoke of instant natural catastrophes along large swaths of the lakeshore. Colonial-period diary entries describe enigmatic "globes of light" or, conversely, rolling waves of palpable blackness that engulfed the region in utter obscurity. A lieutenant governor of Upper Canada, an experienced traveler of the world's sea-lanes, expressed visceral fear of Lake Ontario, whose weather had an evil personality that "could change with strange suddenness."

In the context of such disturbing reports, the sinking of the *Hamilton* and *Scourge* can be viewed as part of a greater regional phenomenology. Vortex researcher Hugh Cochrane has ventured to theorize that the supernatural vicissitudes of Lake Ontario even determined the wary way war was waged there: "In each encounter both sides were eager to break off as quickly as possible and return to the safety of their ports. As the commanders were quick to point out when questioned about this, 'Certain conditions on this lake were not favorable to such action.'"

"'Certain conditions?'" Or something unnatural?

Certain conditions, it is clear, were not favorable to the *Hamilton* and *Scourge*. Maybe they were top-heavy with cannon weight. Maybe they should have taken in sail even though the night was dead calm and action was imminent with the British, potentially at a moment's notice. Maybe they simply exemplify the danger that lies in changing a vessel's name. (*Hamilton*, certainly, was a particularly unlucky renaming—four ships named *Hamilton* have sunk on the Great Lakes, the U.S. Navy's War of 1812 schooner being the first.) Maybe it was all of the above, a confluence of ill omen and risky seacraft consigning a pair of luckless vessels to abrupt eradication.

As the years went by, ships plying the lake came to be fearful of nights when the fog rises thickly and the chill bites deeply. For these are the nights when they seem most likely to appear—a pair of glowing ghost ships, war craft under full sail, gun ports opened and cannon to the ready. Lanterns in the rigging illumine spectral sailors on deck, grim-faced and silent, awaiting the moment of battle. But the moment never comes, and the twin phantoms suddenly keel over and sink amid a cacophony of screaming, dying men. And once again, the *Hamilton* and *Scourge* are gone.

If they were merely the dim echoes of violent death long past, the sighting of the two ghost ships would simply be frightening yet undeniably fascinating. Unfortunately, the appearance of the sister specters bodes foul fortune, a sad fact that canny sailors soon learned the hard way—the fatal way.

* * *

These are the ghosts, and the lake is the cemetery from which they emanate, but much time would pass before anyone succeeded in determining just where their unmarked graves are. In the early 1970s Dr. Daniel Nelson, an independent researcher operating under the auspices of the Royal Ontario Museum, cross-referenced obscure clues buried in Royal Navy logbooks and managed to pinpoint the location of the famous pair of shipwrecks. Magnetometer scans confirmed his detective work.

In 1975 a tethered remotely operated vehicle (TROV) descended into the icy depths and provided a television camera close-up of the *Hamilton*—the closest look any human eyes had had of the craft in nearly two centuries. "As we sat transfixed before the screen," said Nelson, the

"TROV panned slowly across spars, a rudder, the ship's gig, some remains of human skeletons."

The National Geographic Society spearheaded a multiorganization initiative to survey the discovery using both video and still photography. Both wrecks stand on the lake floor nearly upright (and both are consistent in their slight tilt to port). Project archaeologists observed that "the ships looked much the way they would have when they sank, preserved by the cold waters of the lake." In the blurred glare of artificially lit deepwater photography, the ancient goddess Diana glowed, vigilant as ever, a shockingly human figure in the cold black depths. And down there, too, stared Nelson, forever affixed at the fore of his confiscated and condemned ship. It was, as one shipwreck historian mused about the *Scourge* wreck, "as if the ship was still prepared to sail into action against the British fleet."

Through the years, recurrent examinations of the dual discovery have accompanied advances in underwater archaeology. Legendary undersea explorer Jacques Cousteau sent down a submersible in 1980 and the wrecks' fame grew. Celebrated *Titanic* discoverer Robert Ballard turned his attention to the *Hamilton* and *Scourge* in 1990, three-dimensionally mapping the wreck sites in high resolution with a camera-to-computer feed. An international team headed by Canadian scientists launched an intensive investigation with robotic probes in 2008—the most thoroughly detailed survey of the twin shipwrecks to date. In the near-freezing freshwater depths, free from the ravages of sea salt and wood-devouring oceanic organisms, they are remarkably well preserved. They stand nearly upright, still manned by their skeletal crews. "The *Hamilton* and *Scourge* were fully laden, ready for action in the War of 1812," said Tim Legate, president of Save Ontario Shipwrecks. "They're incredible time capsules from that era. There are still sabers tied to the rail and skeletons all over."

As representatives of their moment in warship history, the *Hamilton* and *Scourge* are the most pristine examples yet to be found anywhere. They enjoy the status of World Heritage Sites by United Nations decree. Yet since the time of their discovery they have remained in a complicated jurisdictional limbo. Somewhat surprisingly, the U.S. Navy signed over the formal ownership of the wrecks to the Royal Ontario Museum in 1979. The museum soon turned the title over to the nearby city of Hamilton, Ontario. Ambitious plans to raise and study the wrecks came to nought, beset by bureaucracy and daunting costs. By 2005 the *Toronto Globe and Mail* was reporting a troubling "upsurge of interest in the *Scourge* and *Hamilton* . . . sparked by evidence that unauthorized divers have visited their underwater grave." The newspaper lamented that the sunken warships, home to "the skulls and bones of dozens of American sailors," remain "at the mercy of looters . . . as the federal government, the City of Hamilton and private organizations wrangle over what to do with them."

The Canadian government responded by passing the Ontario Heritage Act in 2006, requiring a special license (and threatening stiff punishment) for any scuba diver wishing to visit, or operate research equipment around, the *Hamilton*, the *Scourge*, and another famous shipwreck, the *Edmund Fitzgerald*, which was claimed by Lake Superior in 1975. "Scuba diving thieves around the world are destroying wrecks for bragging rights, coffee table displays and internet auction profits," reported the Canadian News Network; "the sites need special protection because they contain human remains and must be treated with care and respect."

* * *

They lie beneath the surface, the final resting place of the U.S. Navy's own. Above the surface, their ghosts still haunt the waves of the mysterious lake, and woe to any whose wake they cross. The *Cayuga*, that grand old Great Lakes passenger steamer, offers a cautionary example. As the sun sank on a cloud-thick Lake Ontario evening in 1942, several *Cayuga* crewmen were loitering on the fantail when they spied the two ghost ships radiating eerie phosphorescence astern. Suddenly and simultaneously, the pair of phantoms sank. As the witnesses recounted their odd experience, the *Cayuga's* ancient steward warned them of what lay in store.

When dawn came, the old steward was dead, the victim of what he himself had prophesied.

For he knew, as all old sailors on that perilous lake know, that if the ghosts of the *Hamilton* and *Scourge* cross your ship's wake and go under, it means one grim thing: soon, one of your crew will die.

A Hero Remains Forever

Bold, resourceful, imbued with fighting spirit, Stephen Decatur embodied the youthful élan of the early U.S. Navy and set a template for heroism that to this day inspires those who wear the uniform. The first great American naval hero after John Paul Jones, Decatur enjoyed a meteoric career steeped in adventure and glory. When his life was tragically cut short, the entire nation mourned. Congress adjourned on the day of his funeral, and official Washington from the president on down flocked to the service. In his diary John Quincy Adams lamented the passing of a hero who had galvanized the country and had "illustrated its history and given grace and dignity to its character in the eyes of the world," a man "as dauntless as breathed in this nation, or on the earth."

Decatur, as they say, is gone but not forgotten. Yet he is not only not forgotten, he is not really gone, either. For the restless spirit of one of the Navy's finest still maintains residency at Decatur House, the stately home where he lived all too briefly and died all too soon. The house is of historical significance. It is of architectural significance. And it also happens to have the reputation of being one of the most haunted places in Washington, D.C.

Heroes come and go with the shifting vagaries of generations. But some heroes remain forever—in Stephen Decatur's case, quite literally.

He came from good seafaring stock. His paternal grandfather was a French naval officer; his father, Stephen Sr., was an American naval officer of some renown in the Revolutionary and early Federal periods. Stephen Decatur Jr. was born in 1779, and the sea called to him early, despite his mother's earnest attempts to steer him toward a safer career on land. He received his commission as a U.S. Navy midshipman in 1798, and he took to the service with natural ease and abundant enthusiasm. Handsome, strapping, brave, gifted with innate leadership qualities that inspired his peers, Decatur rose rapidly through the ranks.

Early on, he demonstrated a willingness (expected in officers and gentlemen of his day) to take matters of honor seriously. He fought his first duel in 1799, against a merchant captain who had slighted the Navy. It was pistols at dawn, and Decatur, a crack shot, managed to wound rather than kill his adversary, thereby satisfying honor yet sparing a life. Decatur soon was involved in another such showdown, this time serving as the second to a midshipman who got into a scuffle with the secretary to the British governor of Malta. The Englishman was killed in the ensuing duel, and the governor cried out for a murder trial. The U.S. Navy hustled the two officers home.

But Decatur was soon back in the Mediterranean. In 1804, commanding the schooner *Enterprise*, he became part of Commo. Edward Preble's squadron in the war against the Tripolitan pirates. The fight had not been going well. The pasha of Tripoli had succeeded in capturing the USS *Philadelphia*, a thirty-six-gun frigate, the previous October after she had foundered on rocks while on blockade duty. The American warship was now anchored inside Tripoli Harbor buttressing the defenses of the Barbary pirates' nest. The mission was clear: infiltrate the harbor, destroy the ship, and get out with minimal loss of life. Lieutenant Decatur eagerly volunteered. His *Enterprise* had captured a Tripolitan ketch, which offered a means of entering the hostile harbor undetected. Commodore Preble approved the plan.

Disguised as Maltese mariners and using a Sicilian harbor pilot as their front man, Decatur and seventy-five handpicked men sailed into the pirates' lair on February 17, 1804. They were right alongside the *Philadelphia* before the Tripolitans realized their identity; the alarm shouts came too late. The Americans swarmed over the side. With fist and cutlass and ferocity they recaptured the *Philadelphia* in five minutes without firing a single shot. They put her to the torch and escaped amid the angry fire of Tripolitan shore batteries and gunboats. Twenty Tripolitans had perished in the deck melee; the remainder ended up overboard, except for one taken prisoner. The mission had succeeded without a single American life lost. Decatur, second to board the *Philadelphia* and the last to leap from her burning hull, enjoyed a wave of praise. Lord Nelson himself lauded "the most bold and daring act of the age."

Soon the rising hero was involved in another "bold and daring act." During the August 1804 bombardment of Tripoli, Decatur, now in command of a gunboat squadron, received the terrible news that his younger brother, Lt. James Decatur, USN, had been murdered by the Turkish captain of a Tripolitan gunboat. The treacherous captain had surrendered his vessel only to shoot young Decatur in the head when he came aboard to formally claim the prize. The older brother's sorrow was mixed with fury at the outrage; the larger battle now became a matter of personal vengeance as well.

Stephen Decatur took ten of his men and hunted down and boarded the Tripolitan craft; he himself was first over the rail. The deck immediately became the scene of bloody and ferocious close-quarters combat. Through acrid smoke, amid war shouts and clanging steel and booming pistol shots, Decatur spied his quarry: the deceitful captain who had killed his brother. Swinging his cutlass, Decatur hacked his way through to the Turk. The Turk thrust at him with a boarding pike. Decatur parried and slashed. The pike shot forward. Decatur evaded it and sliced down hard on its point, endeavoring to break it. But it was his own cutlass that broke, right at the hilt. Weaponless now, Decatur stood firm, using his arm to deflect the pike. The Turk's weapon found its mark, piercing Decatur's arm and chest. Decatur still refused to give in, ripping the pike from his own flesh and wrestling the Turk for it. They fell in a tangle to the deck, with Decatur atop the Turk.

The rival crews surrounded them, vying to assist. A Tripolitan's scimitar blade sang through the air in a deadly arc for the back of Decatur's head. Quarter Gunner Reuben James—a veteran of Truxtun's *Constellation* crew and the celebrated victories over *L'Insurgente* and *La Vengeance*, a participant in Decatur's burning of the *Philadelphia*, and a victim that day of two serious wounds already—threw himself forward to intercept the scimitar blade. Reuben James took a gash to the head and saved the life of Stephen Decatur. Remarkably, the brave gunner survived and went on to share in many of Decatur's future adventures.

But Decatur still had to survive this particular adventure. The big Turk had wrestled his way on top and was now crushing his American foe beneath him. Holding Decatur down with one hand, the Turk reached into his sash with the other and unsheathed a curved *yataghan* knife designed for close-in killing. As the knife came down, Decatur freed his left hand

and grabbed the Turk's wrist, then freed his right hand and drew his own pistol. A shot rang out, and the Turk fell back dead—with a certain poetic justice by a pistol ball, retribution for the pistol ball with which he had slain Decatur's brother.

All twenty-four members of the Tripolitan gunboat's crew were killed or wounded; the Americans suffered four wounded. "I find hand to hand is not child's play," recounted Decatur; "'tis kill or be killed." What would have been condemned as a rash, emotionally driven act of foolhardiness had it failed instead became a bold and exemplary victory. Decatur's brother was avenged, and Decatur's star continued to rise. Promoted in recognition for his *Philadelphia* exploit, he became (and remains), at twenty-five years of age, the youngest captain in U.S. Navy history. Various frigate commands ensued along with, in 1806, marriage to Susan Wheeler, the beautiful daughter of the mayor of Norfolk, Virginia. In addition to his ship commands, Captain Decatur handled many shore duties as well—overseeing gunboat construction, supervising the Gosport Navy Yard, and, in 1808, a task he sought assiduously to avoid: serving as a member on the court-martial of Capt. James Barron.

Barron had been a sort of father figure back in Decatur's early midshipman days. Now he was on trial for dereliction of duty in the notorious *Chesapeake-Leopard* affair. The frigate USS *Chesapeake* had just put out from Hampton Roads on a course for the Mediterranean (where Barron was to be commodore) when the British frigate *Leopard* halted her on June 22, 1807. Asserting that Royal Navy deserters were on the *Chesapeake*, the *Leopard*'s captain demanded the right to search the ship. Barron refused to permit a search of a sovereign American vessel, but he also failed to prepare the *Chesapeake* for the imminent hostility. The *Leopard* fired on the American ship, wounding twenty men and killing four. The *Chesapeake* was forced to strike her colors, and the British boarding party seized four of her crewmen (only one of whom turned out actually to be a deserter from the king's navy). The ignominious act inflamed Americans; a hue and cry arose that would echo all the way to the opening guns of the War of 1812. After a court of inquiry, Barron was court-martialed, found guilty of negligence in not clearing for action, and suspended from the Navy for five years.

With his career derailed and a wife and five daughters to support, Barron became a crushed and embittered man. And he considered Decatur one of the main court members responsible for the verdict. Decatur had tried to recuse himself precisely because he had already formed a strong (negatively prejudicial) opinion prior to the proceedings. Thus were sown seeds of animosity that would bear tragic fruit thirteen years hence.

But in the meantime, the grand swirl of events continued apace, continually offering Decatur opportunities for further glory. He achieved one of the significant early naval victories in the War of 1812, commanding the frigate *United States* in a pitched battle against the British frigate *Macedonian* on October 25, 1812. Outmaneuvering and outsmarting his adversary, Decatur pummeled the *Macedonian* until her masts were gone, her cannon useless, and her decks awash in blood. The 24-pounders of the *United States* had fired with such well-coordinated relentlessness that the British, seeing a great wall of flame, thought the American ship was on fire. Toward the end of the war Decatur suffered a rare loss when he attempted to slip the frigate *President* past the British blockade on January 14, 1815. Even in defeat he was admirably courageous. Chased by four British ships, he managed to disable one of them before finally being cornered and bombarded into submission. The Navy Department praised Decatur's "brilliant actions . . . even in the moment of surrendering your ship to an enemy's squadron of vastly superior force."

The war with the British had barely ended when another Barbary war began heating up, this time thanks to the ravages and ransom demands of the bey of Algiers. Decatur was dispatched to the Mediterranean in May 1815 in command of a nine-ship squadron. By the end of June he had captured two Algerian warships and had engaged in fighting that had seen the death of an Algerian admiral. Decatur delivered stern terms at Algiers and secured a commitment to indemnify American ship losses and return all American prisoners. It was a historic and groundbreaking treaty, and though, as Decatur himself noted, it was "dictated at the mouth of a cannon," it was a treaty nonetheless. Subsequent calls at Tunis and Tripoli brought similar agreements. Decatur's show of force had brought an end to long years of Mediterranean brigandage, and he returned to a grateful America, a new chorus of acclamations, and a new nickname: "Conqueror of the Barbary Pirates."

President James Madison and Congress led the national outpouring of praise for America's great naval hero. Decatur was cheered and fêted throughout the land. At a banquet in his honor in April 1816, he raised his glass and made a toast that itself became legendary: "Our country. In her intercourse with foreign nations, may she always be in the right, but our country, right or wrong."

Decatur was the current star ascendant *ne plus ultra* in the naval ranks, and one of the most distinguished appointments possible now came his way, courtesy of Secretary of the Navy Benjamin Crowninshield. The secretary appointed Decatur to the recently created three-man Board of Navy Commissioners in December 1815. The powerful and influential board was an advisory body that answered directly to the secretary and provided him with naval expertise. To be invited to sit on this board was a rare and supreme honor for an officer, his ultimate validation, in a sense.

The board was headquartered in Washington, and the Decaturs relocated to the capital city with style. They purchased land at the northwest corner of President's Park, across from the White House, and set out to build their dream home. Benjamin Henry Latrobe, the eminent architect who had designed the Capitol and other significant Washington edifices, was commissioned to create the Decaturs' house. Decatur instructed Latrobe to design a residence for "impressive entertainments." The elegant three-story brick Federal mansion, completed in 1818, became a focal point of the Washington social scene. The dashing naval hero and his lovely, refined wife became the toast of the city. An invitation to a lavish party at Decatur House was not to be missed. Susan Decatur was emerging as one of the capital's most popular hostesses. Stephen Decatur was involved in important work for the Navy Department by day and enjoying his celebrity status by night. Life was good.

Then the past came knocking. James Barron was back. Through years of destitution, of attempts at merchant seamanship and inventing, of roaming from country to country in search of a new start, Barron had more and more seen one man as the principal author of all his woes, and that man was the wildly successful Stephen Decatur. Barron had been in Denmark in 1813 when his suspension from the Navy expired. Too penniless to make the voyage home at that time, he finally managed to return in 1818 and started lobbying strenuously for a naval command. But many in the service, Decatur included, saw the delay in Barron's return—and thus his failure to serve his country during the War of 1812—as yet another mark against him. His entreaties and protests to the Navy Department fell on deaf ears.

To Barron, the earlier injustice of his original sentence was now compounded. In that vexed state he was vulnerable to the scheming of his old friend, Capt. Jesse Elliott, who had his own reasons to loathe Decatur.

Elliott filled Barron's ears with poisonous insinuations that Decatur was the main obstacle to Barron's attempts to regain a command. Decatur was, in fact, leery of Barron's abilities at this point, but he was far from being alone in that opinion. Meanwhile Elliott helped conflate Decatur into the role of Barron's personal Satan. From 1819 to 1820 a letter-writing war between Barron and Decatur grew increasingly hotter.

Decatur wrote, "I should regret the necessity of fighting with any man; but in my opinion, the man who makes arms his profession is not at liberty to decline an invitation."

Barron replied, "There may be cases of such extraordinary and aggravated insult and injury received by an individual as to render an appeal to arms on his part absolutely necessary. . . . You have hunted me out, have persecuted me with all the power and influence of your office."

Decatur wrote, "If we fight, it must be of your seeking. . . . I shall pay no further attention to any communication you may make to me, other than a direct call to the field."

At that, Barron threw down the fateful gauntlet: "Whenever you will consent to meet me on fair and equal grounds, that is, such as two honorable men may consider just and proper, you are to view this as that call."

The Decaturs' calendar was full as usual in March 1820. When they hosted a gala reception for President Monroe's soon-to-be-wed daughter, several guests noticed that their host appeared at times preoccupied, at other times fawningly attentive to his wife. Two nights later the Decaturs attended Secretary of State John Quincy Adams' dinner dance. Swept up in these lofty social engagements, Susan Decatur was impervious to her husband's recent activities: seeing to their financial affairs, readying his will. If, on their return from the dance, she saw him standing and staring distractedly out the second-floor parlor window, she probably attributed it to grappling over some naval-policy complexity or merely pre-bedtime musings. She would not have known the real reason, for he had assiduously avoided telling her what was to transpire in the morning.

He rose early, bid her farewell, and walked down Pennsylvania Avenue to Beale's Hotel, where he breakfasted with friends. Afterward they climbed into a carriage and rode out to the Bladensburg Dueling Grounds just beyond the city.

Many an affair of honor between Washingtonian gentlemen had been settled at the dueling grounds. The creek that ran through it was known as Blood Run. Decatur and his men met Barron and his men. It was to be pistols at eight paces at 9 AM. The eight paces amounted to a chivalrous concession on Decatur's part; it was the shortest allowable dueling distance and a boon to the inferior shot. Decatur, a far better marksman than the nearsighted Barron, would have been at greater advantage at the more standard ten paces or farther. As the distance was measured and the duelists took their places, Barron said to Decatur that he hoped they might be better friends if ever they met in the next world. Decatur answered, "I have never been your enemy, sir."

The count of three was shouted: "Pre-sent! One! Two—"

Pistol fire rocked the morning stillness.

It was said that the shots erupted at precisely the same second, so that only one shot was heard.

Decatur, as in his earlier duel, intended to wound, not kill, thereby serving honor yet sparing a life. He shot Barron in the hip as intended. Barron likewise aimed for the hip, and likewise hit his mark. Both duelists fell to the ground. Barron would survive his wound. Decatur would not.

Doctors on hand rushed to the bleeding adversaries. "I am mortally wounded," said Decatur, ". . . and wish that I had fallen in defense of my country."

Friends got him into a carriage and took him home. Decatur did not want his wife to see him in that state and entreated that she be whisked upstairs before he was brought inside. He was carried to his first-floor bedroom and made comfortable, and Susan Decatur, distraught and hysterical, was finally allowed to join him. As the terrible news spread, thousands of Washingtonians filed past the first-floor window to pay their respects to the dying hero. His final hours were filled with ever-intensifying pain. At 10 PM on March 22, 1820, Stephen Decatur, aged forty-one, died in the dream house he and his wife had lived in for only fourteen months.

* * *

Years went by. President's Park became Lafayette Square, and a city gradually grew up around Decatur House. Susan rented it out for several years, and a series of foreign dignitaries and U.S. secretaries of state occupied it at various times. She sold the house in 1836 and it remained in private hands until 1956. The first private residence to be built on what became Lafayette Square was also the last remaining private residence there when the house passed into the control of the National Trust for Historic Preservation. Since the 1960s it has been open to the public as a museum.

And it has long had the notoriety of being vividly and vociferously haunted. Many have resided at Decatur House, but it is said that the original occupant never left. In terms of spectral activity, "It has always been a lively house," said a Stephen Decatur House and Museum representative, "and it stays that way today."

Since the year after he died, Stephen Decatur's ghost has been seen standing at the second-floor parlor window, staring up Connecticut Avenue. So common have the sightings been that a good deal of bogus lore has arisen, erroneous information that continues to be perpetuated by ill-informed ghost-tour guides and in the ghostly literature. The story that a first-floor window in Decatur House was bricked over to stop the ghost from appearing at it, for instance, is entirely false. The first-floor window had been bricked in when the house was originally constructed. Bricked-in windows were a Federal Period architectural flourish. The upstairs window preferred by Decatur's ghost remains filled with glass, not brick, and is an extremely haunted spot.

To stand at the window where Decatur's ghost holds his recurrent vigils is to feel a frisson of unease; yet there is a simultaneous, contrasting thrill, the fleeting sense that one of naval history's most famous figures has just brushed your shoulder. But the window is not the sole ectoplasmic power spot at Decatur House; the nearby second-floor stairway landing— a tight, claustrophobic area—exudes a palpable air of death. Stories abound regarding the space between Decatur's window and this landing—stories about footsteps, about disembodied voices at night, about inconsolable weeping. The area around the door to the courtyard likewise is infamously haunted, and the first-floor room where Decatur breathed his last breath still radiates a disturbing sorrow.

Some speculate that Decatur's ghost constantly relives the hours preceding his death: gazing pensively out the window the night before, slipping out the door early the next morning, returning to die amid wailing and tears. If this theory is true, it supports another theory that Decatur's phantom is one of many sad souls that haunt the former Bladensburg Dueling Grounds. More than fifty duels offered blood sacrifice to the earth there, and the area teems with dark, humanoid shapes drifting about ethereally. The least little sound causes the ghosts to vanish immediately, scattering to other haunts until the coast is clear.

If Decatur's ghost cavorts among them, he always comes home to die again. Interest in Decatur House's supernatural blandishments has remained unabated over the years. Ghost investigation television shows and area ghost-hunting societies continue to make the pilgrimage. And for good reason. In a city with more than its share of alleged paranormal activity, Decatur House stands out as a salient spectral hotspot. A shockingly vivid manifestation of Decatur occurred in 2007. The witness, a member of the Decatur House and Museum staff, agreed to be interviewed if her identity was not revealed.

"I've never had a parapsychological experience before," she said. "I don't believe that sort of thing.... But I saw a man." A man who wasn't there.

The museum was closed; there were only a few personnel left in the building at that point, and no one was unaccounted for. The witness was in a third-floor office with two open doors—one to the side of her, the other in front and facing into another office, allowing for the sort of room-to-room conversation now going on between the witness and another staffer across the way. Suddenly someone, something, was hovering in the witness's periphery, in the side entrance. "I was sitting upstairs talking . . . when out of the corner of my eye a man appeared in the doorway."

The witness said she would never forget the pure, primeval shock of the moment. "I jumped back in my chair. There was nobody up there with us at all." But right there, standing a mere few feet away and staring right at her, "was a guy. He had dark hair, a dark top and light trousers.... When I think about it I get goose-bumps."

And then he was gone. He simply disappeared. "It was so profound. I can't talk about it even now without chilling over." For the witness it was, understandably, a transformative moment. Yet for all the uncanniness of the incident, there was nothing particularly threatening about the ghost. "It wasn't scary, exactly; it was just very startling."

Hers was a shockingly lucid encounter, but anyone who works at Decatur House can speak of the abundant signs, the spooky ambience, the voices, the weird noises, the overall sense of the otherworldly permeating these historic walls.

"No one really likes to stay here late," one staffer remarked. "When it gets eerie and you realize you're here by yourself, you get out in a hurry."

But you're never really here entirely by yourself. You are, in fact, in most illustrious company.

A Fatal, Perfidious Brig

Come listen all ye sailors bold.
Come listen unto me,—
I'll sing you of a cruel deed;
A bloody tragedy.

Come listen landsmen, one and all,
Come listen unto me,
I'll make you bless your lucky stars
You've never gone to sea.
          —"The Somers: A Ballad" (1843)

She was an ill-conceived craft, beautiful and doomed. Ignominy was her fate, an ignominy born of events evil and morbid—events that forever would attach her name to one of the blackest chapters in the saga of the U.S. Navy.

They named her after Master Commandant Richard Somers, who had been blown to bits, along with his entire crew, when his ketch exploded at Tripoli in 1804. The U.S. brig *Somers* was sleek and racy—and top-heavy with too much sail for her slender build. Her design offered speed, but it likewise invited trouble. And trouble was her destiny.

She was 100 feet long and 25 feet abeam, and anyone more than four feet, ten inches tall had to duck constantly belowdecks. Above, the *Somers* was flush-decked, sporting a single deck without any varying height forward or aft; officers and crew alike were on the same level. Such leveling can be a dangerous thing, a dire threat to the requisite hierarchy of the high seas.

Lightweight, thin-skinned, and armed nonetheless with ten 32-pound carronades, the *Somers* was too small, really, for her purpose, which was to take a motley assemblage of unruly teenage males and mold them into sailors.

The naval tradition of old held that there was no better training methodology than the time-honored "school of the ship," quite literally learning the ropes at sea. But lubberly young recruits tended to get in the way during the perilous hustle and bustle on deck; they were at best a distraction, at worst a danger. So the Navy decided to try something new: a vessel built specifically for educational purposes. Thus did the cursed craft called *Somers* come into being at the New York Navy Yard in April 1842.

She was to be a floating school in which the enlisted rabble would learn the intricacies of seamanship, and the midshipmen—the future leaders of the Navy—would cultivate seamanship along with book learning. When the Navy looked for a commanding officer who embodied the unique blend of qualities necessary for disciplining, uplifting, and educating a shipload of high-spirited adolescents, eyes turned to Cdr. Alexander Slidell Mackenzie. He appeared to be the ideal candidate. And he recently had become available, though admittedly not under the most encouraging circumstances. He was a man of letters, a published author. He was piously religious. And, though soft-spoken and gentle of manner when mingling in society, he had a reputation as a stern, even cruel, disciplinarian at sea. Indeed, Mackenzie seemed unusually ardent regarding discipline.

Mackenzie's published works included a couple of popular travelogues, *A Year in Spain* and *Spain Revisited*. On his Iberian wanderings during extended shore leaves, the author/officer had witnessed a hanging, which so enthralled him that he felt the urge to attend yet another execution, this time a death by garroting. He breathlessly described it as "a spectacle full of horror and painful excitement, still I determined to witness it. I felt sad and melancholy, and yet, by a strange perversion, I was willing to feel moreso."

This prim, grim little man of strange perversions was known as a ruthless administrator of "cruel, unnecessary and unjust punishment." As first lieutenant on the *Independence*, Mackenzie had ordered that a luckless Marine receive a dozen lashes—the maximum allowable—for having disposed of orange peels improperly. Twelve lashes: 108 gore-spewing, pustulant welt lines crisscrossing the flesh in a horrid roadmap of permanent scarring. The cat-o'-nine-tails, that vile whip that turned a man's back into oozing raw meat, saw robust and liberal use wherever Mackenzie was in command. From the *Independence* to the *Dolphin* to the *Fairfield*, he left bloodstained decks and embittered sailors in his wake. His modest literary success may have inordinately impressed his naval superiors, but before the mast Mackenzie was known not as an author but as a tyrant "noted for his cruelty to the men for small offenses and trifling accidents."

That Mackenzie was well connected was an undeniable boon to his erratic naval career. His brother-in-law was the great Commo. Matthew Calbraith Perry, and Perry it was who gave Mackenzie the *Somers* assignment. At that point, the thirty-nine-year-old Mackenzie was sorely in need of a new command. His previous one had ended in shame when he took the newly built steam frigate USS *Missouri* and ran her aground. Attempts to place blame elsewhere failed, and Mackenzie was relieved of command. Then came the *Somers*, a golden opportunity tailor-made for the scholar-officer's talents, a fresh chance most fortunately timed. But what seems at first to be a blessing can turn out to be a bane.

Mackenzie swiftly proved what sort of iron-handed disciplinarian he would be as the floating academy's headmaster. For the worst offenses—stealing, desertion, and such—Mackenzie's law was enforced by the dreaded cat. Other crimes were punishable by the cat's junior partner in pain—the colt, a three-thonged rope whip. The majority of the recruits aboard the *Somers* were mere lads between fourteen and eighteen years old. Before they ever even put out to sea, these boys were subjected to 422 whippings for such offenses as swearing, spitting, and uncleanliness. The violence-enforced strictness continued through the devil brig's shakedown cruise to Puerto Rico and back.

Soon, she would embark on her first official mission, delivering dispatches to a Navy vessel patrolling off the African coast. The ostensible mission was pretense, of course; the true goal of the voyage was to train the fledgling crew in the ways of the sea. The *Somers* was intended to accommodate about 90 souls, and would be cramped quarters at that. But as she made ready to set sail for Africa, her ranks had swollen unhealthily to 120; ships eager to get rid of burdensome apprentice seamen had been dumping them on the new school ship with zeal. The officer contingent—Mackenzie, his assisting senior officers/teachers, and his midshipmen—numbered twelve. Mackenzie had handpicked most of them, and many were related to him through his auspicious connections—twelve officers bound by overlapping cliques of family ties and rank.

But there was to be a thirteenth officer. He came into their midst against their wishes, and against his own.

The thirteenth officer was a dark, brooding eighteen-year-old with a weird, off-kilter eye; old salts might have called him "swivel-eyed." That feature marked him, according to seafaring lore, as a Jonah. A recent failed surgical attempt to correct this unfortunate strabismus had left the thirteenth officer with an even more disturbingly crooked stare. His penchant for menacing, enigmatic half-smiles only added to his aura of baleful portent.

A student of the numerologically arcane might discern some occult significance in the fact that this evil-omened thirteenth officer had thirteen letters in his name, and that his orders to report came on August 13. Regardless of such mystical considerations, it was clear from the outset that the arrival of Philip Spencer on Mackenzie's brig created a volatile alchemy. From the moment the new acting midshipman reported for duty and shook hands with his new commander, the fate of the *Somers* was locked between two irreconcilably antagonistic personalities. And some foul outcome, some satanic inevitability, threatened like the taunting whisper of wind in the rigging.

For Philip Spencer, the ne'er-do-well son of Secretary of War John Canfield Spencer, was the walking embodiment of all that the priggish, rigid Mackenzie loathed. Mackenzie was resolutely dogmatic in his piety; Spencer was enthusiastically immoral in his outlook and habits. Mackenzie was abstemious and temperate; Spencer drank and smoked with sensuous abandon—not yet out of his teens, he already was notoriously debauched. Mackenzie was a stickler for the trappings of rank, propriety, and decorum; Spencer sneered with disdain at his peers and mingled with whom he pleased.

Mackenzie was a careerist; Spencer vociferously loathed the Navy. He was on the *Somers* only because his father had placed him there after a string of other failed attempts to tame his obstreperous, embarrassing offspring. Two forays into the college milieu had fizzled inconclusively. It was not that young Spencer lacked intelligence; he emerged from his checkered academic career grounded in the liberal arts, including a rudimentary proficiency in foreign and classical languages. But while he was competent enough to interpret the classics, his preferred reading matter leaned toward the lurid, the sensational. His favorite volume was *The Pirate's Own Book*. He dreamed of living the life of a freebooter, wild and free on the open seas—a fast ship beneath his feet, a loyal crew, a hold full of plunder, the wind at his back, and lusty wenches adorning his arms.

He also loved the romance and mystique of clubbish ritual, of ciphers and secret handshakes and cabalistic quasi-mysticism. Before his collegiate career foundered, Spencer managed to help launch a fraternal order that survives on campuses to this day as Chi Psi Fraternity. Its brethren still raise their mugs to toast their wayward cofounder, singing hearty drinking songs in his honor and performing clandestine ceremonies in memory of his ill-fated life.

In short, Spencer fantasized about sea roving and loved the concept of belonging to an elite cadre with its own unique codes, practices, and traditions. But he hated being in the Navy. Far too much was expected of him; there were too many rules, too many restrictions on his imagination and wanton hedonism. His prior Navy assignment with the Brazilian Squadron had ended with a drunken brawl involving an English officer and sundry locals of Rio de Janeiro. Arrested and ordered aboard the USS *Potomac* to be whisked homeward in shame with all dispatch, Spencer gave full voice to his caged rage. "I remember well his valedictory, so passionately uttered," recounted a shipmate. "He damned fleet and flag . . . rounding off with oaths and the threat to be 'even with them.'"

Being the son of the secretary of war was enough in 1842 to afford even the most reckless troublemaker a reprieve. For Spencer, just as it was for Commander Mackenzie, the *Somers* was to be another chance. Spencer wasted no time in squandering it, becoming embroiled at the outset in a scheme to smuggle liquor aboard. Mackenzie was not pleased to have to accept this reprobate into his already full wardroom. He tried to get rid of Spencer, but to no avail. The time had come to depart for Hell.

Sailors' superstition, that ancient body of uncannily prescient knowledge passed down through the mist-shrouded ages, is specific in its admonishments about which days are fortuitous for departure and which are not. Tuesday, for example, is considered a terribly unlucky day on which to begin a voyage. The thirteenth day of the month is regarded as the most unfortunate date possible on which to head out.

The *Somers* departed on Tuesday, September 13.

New York Harbor to the Azores. Madeira to the Canary Islands. Tenerife to the Cape Verde Islands. Cape Verde to Cape Mesurada on the West African coast. The overcrowded brig wended her course across the autumnal Atlantic. Three days out of New York, the floggings began; three boys (one of them but thirteen years old) were whipped for the offense of "skulking," or trying to avoid work. Eight days out, nine more floggings, for disobedience and skulking. Nine days out, another flogging for disobedience, a fourteen-year-old this time. Again and again, the cat and the colt lashed out their harsh justice—for impertinence, for sleeping on watch, for uncleanliness, for washing clothes without asking permission first, for dropping tobacco on deck, for not wearing a white hat, for profanity, for spilling tea: forty-three floggings in the first three weeks.

Harsh discipline was the age of sail's pedagogic standard, to be sure, but many even at the time were shocked when the punishment record of the *Somers* was made public: a total of 2,265 lashes ripped into the backs of boys during Mackenzie's command. The record belonged to a fourteen-year-old who over the course of the training cruise received a total of 101 lashes, 87 with the colt and 14 with the cat. By October, discontent was rising among the beleaguered young crew. A shore leave in the lush paradise of Madeira merely made the brutal, cramped shipboard life seem all the more unbearable once it resumed. An underlying surliness was surfacing, and occasionally finding its voice. And the friction between the haughty young officers and the beaten young crew was being exacerbated by a misfit who dared violate the taboo separating the two hierarchical groups: Philip Spencer.

Unpleasant, disrespectful, slovenly, odd—he was the outcast of the wardroom. He was not one of them. They were all faithful to Mackenzie, and Spencer had come to despise the captain. And so the outcast did what an officer is never supposed to do: he abandoned his fellow officers and stooped to socialize with the enlisted men. Spencer broke down the invisible wall and mingled with the common sailors, joked with them, procured brandy and cigars for them. He made himself a clown for their approval, showing off his bizarre talent for putting his jaw out of joint and performing elaborate melodies with its back-and-forth motion. The class debasement in such an insane display shocked and annoyed Mackenzie.

Most dangerous of all, Spencer spoke to the rabble in forbidden ways, savaging and ridiculing the captain, fantasizing about turning pirate, speculating about how, with a few stout fellows, he could commandeer the brig. He was disgruntled, out of his element, slave to an overheated imagination. And he was talking too much, perhaps even violating Article 13 of the Articles of War, which states that "if any person . . . shall utter any seditious and mutinous words, or shall conceive or connive at any mutinous or seditious practices, or shall treat with contempt his superior . . . he shall be punished."

The *Somers* anchored at Monrovia only to learn that the ship to which they were to have delivered dispatches had left the African coast and made for the West Indies. The *Somers* followed in pursuit. And it was on a fateful November night, on course for St. Thomas, that Spencer approached Purser's Steward James Wales and invited him to climb up the foremast with him for a private conversation. If what Wales later testified was true, then it was one incendiary chat.

Spencer tried to recruit Wales to join a murderous plot to take over the ship. Some night soon, in the black hours after midnight, Spencer and his co-conspirators were going to fake a deck fight to lure the watch officer, then heave him overboard. Then they would open the arms chest and cover all the hatches. Spencer would go below and personally slay the captain while he lay sleeping. Then he and his fellow mutineers would go around and kill all the other officers and take over the *Somers*. She was fast, after all, and would make a fine pirate craft.

As for the rest of the crew, if you were with Spencer, then welcome to the buccaneer's life, me hearties. If you were against him, then you'd soon be joining the officers' corpses plummeting into the dark depths.

The steward fearfully pretended to go along, then informed his superiors at the first opportunity. Initially, Commander Mackenzie took the shocking news with a strange stoicism. He merely ordered his first lieutenant, Guert Gansevoort, to watch Spencer closely. Gansevoort later spied Spencer aloft in the foretop having a crude tattoo scraped into his skin by one of the crew. Gansevoort ordered them down. On the Jacob's ladder, Spencer trained his scary, crooked eye on Gansevoort, and a chill ran through the lieutenant. The evil eye stayed fixed on Gansevoort for a long, tense, wordless minute. It was, said Gansevoort, "the most infernal expression I have ever seen upon a human face. It satisfied me at once of the man's guilt."

By sundown, the crowded quarterdeck was the scene of the confrontation that had been brewing since the voyage began.

"I learn, Mr. Spencer, that you aspire to the command of the *Somers*," said Mackenzie.

"Oh, no sir," Spencer replied, smiling.

"Did you tell Mr. Wales, sir, that you had a project to kill the commander, the officers, and a considerable portion of the crew of this vessel, and convert her into a pirate?"

"I may have told him so, sir, but it was in joke."

"You admit then that you told him so?"

"Yes, sir, but in joke . . . it's all a joke."

"This, sir, is joking on a forbidden subject. This joke may cost you your life."

Mackenzie ordered Spencer's sword confiscated and had him clapped in double irons. Bizarre evidence of the mutiny plot quickly mounted: a sketch by Spencer of the *Somers* flying a pirate flag; hearsay regarding Spencer's exceeding interest in the Isle of Pines, a legendary pirate lair west of Cuba; and, most damning, two strange pieces of paper covered with Greek writing. On the first sheet were lists of names categorized as "Certain," "Doubtful," and "To Be Kept *Nolens Volens* [willing or unwilling]." Those sure to join the plot plus those likely to join totaled thirteen potential mutineers. The second sheet placed names with positions at which the men were to be stationed, presumably during the mutiny.

The mood on board was tense; the officers stayed on constant alert, patrolling with cutlass and pistol. Spencer was soon joined aft by another prisoner in irons, one of his alleged co-conspirators, burly, menacing Boatswain's Mate Samuel Cromwell. The mood grew tenser. The officers were tiring, and every little incident seemed to portend a mass uprising by the disgruntled crew. The weary, edgy officers felt the vast emptiness of the surrounding sea and recognized how truly outnumbered they were by the volatile crew. Then the main topgallant mast came down and panic broke out on deck. Sailors rushed aft; it looked initially like an attack to spring Spencer and Cromwell, but the crew had been sent there to help control the damage. Spencer and Cromwell were joined by another alleged mutineer in irons, wizened old Seaman Elisha Small.

Mackenzie was still captain, but fear was now the true commander of the *Somers*. The vessel had never seemed so small. The three prisoners were hard to guard in that diminutive space, and soon another four were in irons as well. The crew was in bad spirits. Fearful that he was about to lose control of his ship, Mackenzie ordered his officers to hold an ad hoc court of inquiry. Thirteen witnesses were brought before the court and questioned. The circumstantial evidence was cobbled together. The accused were never questioned, nor even told that an inquiry was taking place below. The officers came to Mackenzie with their conclusions. Mackenzie, apparently not satisfied, sent them back to deliberate. They came back again, and he sent them below again. Finally, they came to him with the ultimate conclusion, and he sent them back no more.

Mackenzie personally delivered the news to Spencer, Cromwell, and Small: in ten minutes they were going to die.

A shocked Spencer doubled over and began bawling. Mackenzie entreated him to die like an officer and a gentleman. Spencer regained his composure enough to ask, between sobs, "But haven't you formed an exaggerated estimate of the extent of this conspiracy? Aren't you going too far—too fast? Does the law entirely justify you?"

They may as well have been rhetorical questions. Sailors were ordered into three lines, each to haul on one of the three long hanging ropes now draped over the yardarm. Officers brandished cutlasses and stood alongside with orders to cut down any sailor who didn't pull when the signal sounded.

Three nooses were placed around three necks.

"Tell my wife I die an innocent man!" shouted Cromwell.

"Now, brother shipmates," yelled Small, "give me a quick death! Run me up smartly."

Their faces were masked in death shrouds—frock-cloth on Cromwell and Small, a black neckerchief on Spencer. The signal carronade boomed. Officers held cutlasses ready as three lines of sailors surged forward, hauling. Three bodies now dangled in the sky, spasmodically jerking, flailing, choking, dying, swaying to and fro with the rocking of the ship.

Beneath their demented marionette's death dance, Commander Mackenzie stood in full-dress uniform and delivered a sermon to the terrified young crew. He lectured on the grim results of lives sinfully spent as the three men he had just executed dangled above him, ghastly black silhouettes against the afternoon sky. Some boys wept; others dared to glance upward at the corpses swinging from the yardarm and let out nervous giggles. Mackenzie rallied them and ordered them to give three cheers to the American flag.

The sick, Gothic tableau inspired a contemporaneous bard to musings both macabre and cynical:

> The deed is done! That cruel deed—
> "Three cheers" the captain cries,
> "Three cheers" for that dark blood striped flag
> That o'er us mocking flies.

The corpses remained dangling as the crew was piped below to dinner. They dined beneath the dead men dancing in the wind. As daylight waned, the corpses were lowered and readied for burial. Cromwell and Small were sewn into their hammocks; as an officer, Spencer warranted a coffin, in his case a makeshift affair fashioned from a couple of mess chests. The twilight sky grew black and blew up into a storm. The men hastily threw canvas over the dead bodies as the rain pounded down and an angry wind howled. When the squall subsided, they carried out the sea burial in the pitch-black night, lanterns flickering eerily as the bodies were committed to the deep.

> And sad and slow our messmates dead
> We launched into the waves,
> And watched them sink, mid ocean's moans,
> Deep in their watery graves.
>
> O'er them the winds a requiem sing;
> Deep, mournful sounds the blast;
> And shriller hiss the curling waves
> As homeward we speed fast.

The *Somers* arrived at the island of St. Thomas four days later. Could not Mackenzie and his faithful followers have kept the prisoners safely ensconced from any mutinous rescue attempt for a mere four more days? Proper justice could then have been served, the U.S. Constitution not violated, and the prisoners handed over to consular authorities, eventually to receive the proper court-martial that was their right as free-born sons of America. Mackenzie spent the rest of his life defending the rash executions as necessary to save the ship from being overrun by mutineers.

Was Spencer actually planning a mutiny, or was he merely a frustrated fraternity boy drawing pictures and making silly secret-code lists as outlets for his immature fantasy world? Even if he had been serious, did he have the spine necessary to go through with such a ghastly scheme? Whether or not Mackenzie could have stayed the course for four more days, and whether Spencer was a serious threat or merely a seriously foolhardy roué, the world can never know until the sea gives up her dead and the waterlogged, skeletal specters haunting the ocean floor can at last rise up, and walk, and tell their stories to the living.

> Our brig flies like some guilty thing
> Faster, more fast she flies,
> From where the blood of murdered men
> From the deep ocean cries.

On December 14, 1842, thirteen days after the executions and thirteen weeks after departing on her nightmare voyage, the *Somers* arrived back in New York. Mackenzie quickly got to work defending his actions. Applying all his writing skills, he wrote a thirteen-thousand-word report presenting his dubious decision making in the most laudatory possible light. That the *Somers* tragedy became a consuming national scandal of the next several months is the stuff of history. As political factions and the public press debated the affair with tempestuous rancor, Mackenzie stood first before a court of inquiry, then ultimately before a court-martial presided over by thirteen officers.

On the charges of murder and other sundry offenses, the final verdict was "not proved." The court did not brand Mackenzie guilty, that is, but neither did they absolve him as "fully and honorably acquitted." When news of the verdict reached Washington, a fistfight broke out between bereaved, embittered Secretary of War Spencer and Secretary of the Navy Abel Upshur; President John Tyler had to separate the two men.

Three days after the verdict was announced, Richard Leecock, the ship's surgeon aboard the *Somers*—one of the officers who had voted to execute Spencer and the others—sat in the evil brig's berth deck and blew his brains out.

On September 13, 1848—six years to the day after the *Somers* set sail on her fateful voyage—Alexander Slidell Mackenzie, never a robust man, died at the age of forty-seven.

> In vain! In vain! Thou can'st escape,
> Fatal, perfidious bark!
> The stains of blood are on thy deck,
> Thy freight is curses dark!

And the *Somers*? She became a ship of sinister dread, an assignment no Navy man requested or relished. They said she was cursed, that bad luck sailed with her. And soon, as the reported sightings began to accrue, they said she was haunted.

And other hands than flesh and blood
Thou numberest 'mongst the crew;
And a ghostly "mess" thou'lt always hear
Across the ocean blue.

Terror-stricken sailors increasingly reported seeing the ghosts of the
three hanged men swinging from the yardarm.

No! often on that gallows spar
The yardsmen brave will quail,
In the midnight watch at figures three
Unearthly—fleshless—pale.

And they heard the plaintive moaning of the dangling dead men in the
dread blackness of the night.

Strange sounds will float upon the air,
And in the blast will speak;
And round the main-yard arms three ghosts
Will play, and dance, and shriek!

The *Somers* came to be considered such a dreadful assignment that
a sailor headed there could expect great sympathy and concern from his
friends. When Midn. Robert C. Rogers was ordered to report to the devil
brig for blockade-running patrol off Vera Cruz during the Mexican War,
his shipmates consoled him "on a change so regrettable and inauspicious."

"Good-bye and God bless you, my boy," they said. "Get rid of that craft
as soon as you can, for sooner or later she's bound to go to the Devil. Since
the mutiny, damned bad luck goes with her. Keep your eyes skinned. Some
night you'll see Spencer swinging from the yard-arm from which he was
hanged, as he, and the others too, have been seen time and again."

Rogers, who had known Spencer back in the Brazilian Squadron days,
soon became attuned to the malevolent pall that hung over the *Somers*. "At
night especially, when the fierce north wind whistled and moaned through
the spars and the rigging . . . I did not wonder that many of the crew
believed the vessel haunted. I must confess that I have been amazed on
several occasions, in the obscurity of the night, when the topsails were
being reefed and the sails hung loosely and low from the yards, to see

their folds, at times, assume human shapes ... the forms of the suspended mutineers."

Rogers recalled in particular "one nasty, black night" when "it was blowing great guns, and it was necessary to get the vessel under as scant a spread of canvas as possible." The main topmen were supposed to be reefing the topsails, but they were hanging up there paralyzed instead of reining in the canvas. "The clamor of wind and wave was so great that it was impossible to reach the men with the speaking-trumpet," said Rogers. "I was ordered aloft to ascertain why they hesitated to perform a duty usually executed with so much alacrity and skill."

As he ascended, he was engulfed by a demonic miasma of wind, spray, and ear-splitting banshee howls. "I shall never forget that adventure, and the repugnance, if not fear, I experienced. . . . It was pitch-dark, but at intervals the scurrying clouds would open and through the rifts let down enough light to enable me to see the wild waves like so many monsters leaping up to seize me ... a multitude of voices screeched through the rigging as if threatening and reviling me. . . . I reached the top, and ... found the men huddled in the leeward shelter of the mast. . . . I asked the captain of the top why he and his men did not lay out to reef it. Amid that awful din I scarce heard his reply, but followed his finger, pointing to the weather yard-arm."

Rogers looked where the topman was pointing, then shouted, "I see nothing!"

"Spencer and Small!" the topman cried. "Don't you see 'em?"

"I peered through the darkness," Rogers said, "my heart rapidly mounting to my mouth as I recalled the people of that tragedy. . . . My very fears, moving in accord with my imagination, so much excited by all the circumstances of the incident, did really for a moment persuade me that I saw Spencer's ghost."

Rogers managed to muster a modicum of sanity and steered the terrified men through their immediate task of reefing the topsail. On the following day, in the comforting safety of sunlight, Rogers ran into the topman and tried to make light of the previous night's frightful visions.

"All right, sir, all right," the topman replied quietly. "There are things you gentlemen abaft the mainmast don't see, and if you did, why, you wouldn't laugh at them. But mark my words, the brig's doomed; she'll never see port again, and a good many of us will go down with her."

Rogers was shortly afterward captured by Mexican soldiers while attempting a mission on shore. But it was a lucky thing for him, really—it was a good time to be absent from the *Somers*, for the topman's prophecy proved true. On December 8, 1846, less than two weeks after the grim prediction was made, the *Somers* ran into a deadly squall while chasing a possible blockade-runner and sank in less than ten minutes' time. Thirty-two of the seventy-man crew perished along with the ill-fated brig—including the man who had seen her ghosts and had foreseen her watery fate.

> And ill luck, and misfortune dire
> Will follow in thy wake,
> Till the ghastly three, where lie their bones,
> Thy last dark haven make.
>
> Oh! better far to yield her then
> At once unto the dead,
> Than keep the bloody, cursed craft,
> An honest seaman's dread!

*   *   *

And there she lay for 140 years in 110 feet of water—this doomed, morose hull, haunted by three hanged men, one headless suicide victim, and thirty-two brave sailors who went down with her to their eternal sleep. Then, in 1986, an intrepid sea adventurer named George Belcher managed to locate the infamous vessel, using old yellowed charts superimposed on modern navigational data. It was a find, naturally, of profound significance to naval history—and it was a shipwreck, not surprisingly, of pronounced ghostly manifestations.

"We swam down into a murky green sea that got darker and darker the deeper we went," recounted Belcher. "It was like swimming into a tunnel. It was oppressive. But the strange thing was that when we got almost to the bottom where I thought it would be darkest of all, there was a kind of glow. The sand was picking up what little light had made it down that far and reflecting it back, and in the heart of that ghostly glow were the half-buried bones of the *Somers*."

On that dive and subsequent ones with an underwater cameraman, the Belcher crew found themselves in a murky environment co-inhabited by the paranormal. "During our dives on the *Somers*, strange things began to happen," Belcher said. "We had often talked about the *Somers*' reputation as a cursed ship, as a haunted ship. But suddenly, when the weather would turn unusual at the strangest times, or a diver would come from 110 feet below and claim that he heard voices, or that he saw something standing on the bottom, well, we all began to consider the story of the *Somers* ghosts and her curse a little more seriously."

George Belcher's brother and partner in the adventure, Joel Belcher, added, "Intellectually, it's easy to dismiss the stories as pure legend. But when you dive on this shipwreck . . . the water takes on a spooky, diaphanous quality." He recounted an incident in which Chip Matheson, one of the team's top divers, surfaced from a particularly weird and disturbing visit to the shipwreck.

"OK," Matheson had said, "who's the joker who was yelling at me down there?"

Joel Belcher recalled with a shiver, "We looked around at each other—because Chip had been diving on the wreck by himself."

> Sheet home on every cursed spar,
> Set every rag of sail,
> And leave her to the ocean ghouls,
> And demons of the gale!

Hers was a gruesome career marked by cruelty, ill-fortune, and strange death. But despite her many woes, her many evils, something quite positive came about because of the *Somers*. So disastrous was her experimental school ship cruise that the Navy chose to emulate the Army's West Point model rather than risk another. Thus it was the tragedy of the *Somers* that gave birth to the United States Naval Academy.

And the venerable Academy, while succeeding in its mission where the *Somers* failed, nonetheless has something in common with that fatal, perfidious brig: for here, too, there be ghosts.

The Annapolis Anomaly

She came from hearty pioneer stock. Being the seventh daughter, she was imbued with the psychic attunements that can accrue to that place in the birth sequence. Rosa Brant grew to womanhood strong and vigorous. She married Oregon railroad man Jim Sutton and bore him five children. Rosa Brant Sutton's maternal instinct was amplified by her innate extrasensory powers. Many took note of the inexplicable telepathy that existed between the mother and her children. Over the years, in matters both weighty and trivial, Rosa exhibited a remarkable telepathic bond with her daughters. But of all her brood, Rosa always had the most profound mystic connection with Jimmie. He was her firstborn.

When Jimmie was a toddler, for example, she saved him from drowning in a barrel of rainwater—after hearing the warning voice of her own dead father and racing to the barrel mere moments before little Jimmie was beyond rescue. As in so many other instances in which Rosa Sutton displayed an uncanny sensitivity to the sudden, sharp utterances of the dead, there was a witness on hand to verify the mind-boggling and eerie sequence that occurred that day.

One night, out of nowhere, Rosa cried that her brother was dead, cried it repeatedly to her disbelieving husband—disbelieving, that is, until a few hours later when the telegram arrived announcing the brother's death. Rosa likewise predicted, just before it occurred, her mother's demise many miles away—again with witnesses to her disturbing clairvoyance.

But it was her first, her Jimmie, whose pleas from the netherworld she heard loudly and relentlessly until the Sutton mystery became a consuming national fervor. It bound for all time the U.S. Naval Academy with one of the most celebrated and rigorously investigated cases in the annals of psychic phenomena. For Jimmie came to a tragic end as Lt. James N. Sutton Jr., USMC, a young man with a badly beaten face and a bullet in his brain. He lay dying on Naval Academy soil in the predawn blackness of October 13, 1907, in a dark dale between Halligan Hall and Hospital Point. Life seeped from his battered frame there, but his spirit remained (and remains), restless and indignant. It shook the foundations of power; it moaned from the shadows to a mother's ears, and from there to the corridors of justice. It commanded the attention of the public and the press. Even the august *New York Times* agreed that "some of the details of so-called supernatural, or supernormal, occurrences in this case, have been corroborated with such complete evidence that even to the wholly skeptical they remain puzzling to the last degree, entirely inexplicable, indeed."

And thus did the Naval Academy, founded in the wake of the paranormal-infused *Somers* horror, itself become host to the paranormal.

Originally called simply the Naval School, the sea service's equivalent to West Point opened on the grounds of old Fort Severn alongside Annapolis in 1845; in 1850 it became known as the Naval Academy. Except for a four-year evacuation as the Civil War tramped its muddy boots through (during which time the operation temporarily relocated to Rhode Island), the Academy has fulfilled its mission of molding the Navy's future leaders along the banks of the Severn River and College Creek. In those heady early decades of the school's existence, young men from across a young nation dreamed Annapolis dreams. But not all who were accepted made it through. Academy life was rigorous, demanding; intensive studies, training, and hazing all took a toll. The first brutal year "on the Yard" was a weeding-out process. To have been accepted into the Academy was an honor; not to make it through was cause for disappointment, but not necessarily cause for shame. It was damnably tough.

Jimmie Sutton entered the Academy in 1904, a scrappy westerner described as both high-spirited and sensitive, with equal penchants for pugnacity and poetry—in short, brimming with potential. Hazed, hospitalized after a boxing match, falling behind in certain classes, he made it through to 1905 before resigning from the Academy. But he kept his hand in by applying for the Marine Corps officer-training program. Entering the Corps brought him back to the Academy; acceptance into the Marine Corps Application School billeted him back on the Yard.

But this time he would never leave it.

Halligan Hall, that picturesque Annapolis landmark, was home to the Marine Corps barracks and officer-training school in 1907, the antecedent to today's Quantico for Marine officers-to-be. The field between Halligan

Hall and College Creek where fans now fill bleachers to cheer Navy base-ball was in 1907 the Marines' parade ground, and home to thirteen tents housing the young officers in training. The thirteen tents faced the graves of the naval dead, holding eternal sentinel above the waves, on the hill leading up to the hospital. The cemetery was a popular destination to take a lady friend for an amorous tryst.

Carvel Hall, a new and fashionable Annapolis hotel that threw elegant soirées, was a magnet for young swains of both the Navy and Marine per-suasions—and the eligible local ladies for whom they vied. There was a Naval Academy dance, a "middie hop" in the parlance of the day, at Carvel Hall on Saturday night, October 12, 1907. Here, something transpired that within hours would result in violent death. The stories told later would vary, but the conflicting accounts shared some details in common: much liquor, rivalry over a woman, inflamed tempers.

It was well past midnight when the sentry heard shouts and gunshots on the parade ground. Officers were roused, and the news was bad: two Marines had been wounded by another Marine who then shot himself.

Officers and the doctor on duty converged at the body of the shooter lying face down in blood. They rolled him over and lit matches to see bet-ter: bruises on the lip, the cheek, the forehead; gravel ground into the lac-erated nose; a gunshot wound up behind the right ear, residue gunpowder and viscous brain effluvium in the blood.

There was still a slight pulse. But before the stretcher made it up the hill to the hospital, Jimmie Sutton was dead.

As Jimmie's life leaked away in the early morning hours on the East Coast, Rosa Sutton was spending Saturday evening with her daughters in the parlor of the house on Hoyt Street in Portland, Oregon, when she felt a sudden explosion of pain.

"Something has happened to Jimmie!" she screamed.

She felt a blow to the head, then a stab in the heart. "Oh God! Save him!"

Her distraught daughters tried helplessly to comfort her. Then Mr. Sutton arrived home. And Rosa sensed that he had not come through the door alone.

She whispered, "Jimmie is here."

Mr. Sutton said, "Can you stand some bad news?"

Rosa asked what she already knew: "Is Jimmie hurt?"

"He is dead."

The family collapsed in collective despair. But Jimmie was there with them in the parlor. The others couldn't tell, but Rosa saw him plain as day. "You must clear my name," the ghost begged her. "God will give you the means to bring these men to justice."

"Do any of you see Jimmie or hear what he is saying?" Rosa cried. The ghost kept pleading with her: "Mama, they beat me almost to death. I did not know I was shot until my soul went into eternity. They either knocked or struck me in the jaw . . . there is a big lump on the left side. I never had a chance to defend myself."

She repeated his words as the rest of the family listened in horror. A terse telegram from the U.S. Navy soon disputed the ghost's version of the events: "It is reported from Annapolis Lieutenant James M. Sutton committed suicide at 1:20 this morning, Oct. 13, 1907."

Suicide: to the Catholic Suttons that was a cardinal sin, enough to prevent Jimmie from burial in holy ground, enough to keep his soul from eternal rest in Heaven. No wonder, then, that he cried out for vindication. No wonder that his spirit remained restless beyond the corporeal threshold. A reporter arrived at the household of bereavement and, seeking quotes, tactlessly conveyed lurid details of the prevailing account of the occurrence, telling the Suttons that at the dance Jimmie "drank a little too much, on the way home got crazy mad, and blew the whole top of his head off."

Newspapers across America carried banner headlines about the shocking suicide at the Naval Academy. And throughout those awful first four days, the dead son haunted his attuned mother. His ghost was plaintive, articulate, repeatedly pleading, "If you could only see my forehead, you would know how they beat me."

He also told her the gun he had been shot with was *not* his—that his killers had planted it on him.

The other young men involved were together on their story: Sutton had started trouble with them, they unanimously recited. It was all Sutton's fault, and it all culminated with Sutton suddenly turning his rage inward—shooting *himself* in the head.

As suicide scenarios go, it certainly was baroque. To the Navy, it was a matter of case closed. To Rosa Sutton, it was thoroughly unbelievable.

Maternal intuition and spectral visitations were telling her a different version. And for months on end, as the Navy and Marine Corps brass wished she would just go away, Mrs. Sutton pursued her son's case with unflagging doggedness, incorporating family, friends, the press, and any influential allies she could recruit. Bit by bit, she chipped away at the veneer of the military's facile account of the tragedy of October 13, 1907: a supportive witness here, a factual discrepancy there, a growing body of snippets adding up to a compelling case for reexamination of what really had happened that terrible night.

As 1907 turned into 1908, the national press continued to squeeze miles of ink out of the sensational story of the bereaved psychic mother who would not give up her quest to clear her son's name. Eventually, the stories were not just about the ghostly advice she had followed (to the amusement or amazement of readers early on); they began to show an ever-increasing conviction that something was just not right about the official story regarding Sutton's death.

As time passed and the case remained a gaudy part of the national conversation, it inevitably drew the attention of serious scholars of the supernatural. The American Society for Psychical Research, a highly respected organization known for its rigorous spirit of inquiry, healthy skepticism, and scientific methodologies, sent field investigator M. A. Thacher to Portland to dig into the Sutton phenomenon. Soon, his leg-work revealed that Rosa was not the only one who had been visited by Jimmie Sutton's ghost.

Thacher described "friends and relatives of the Sutton family . . . who say that they have seen the 'apparition' of Jimmie since his death." First, there was one of Sutton's sisters, whom Jimmie visited on a train. The sister, Thacher said, "corroborates Mrs. Sutton's statement by saying that Jimmie said he did not kill himself but was murdered, in the manner he is said to have detailed to his mother."

Then Thacher found another witness. "Still another lady, unconnected with the family, and said to be of the highest standing, not a spiritist, reports an apparition of the young officer, in full uniform, not long after his death; the apparition made no statement."

And, most eye-opening of all, there was "a near relative of Mr. Sutton's [who] reported, a few days after Jimmie's death and before she had heard anything about Mrs. Sutton's experiences, that she had had a vision of Jimmie, and that he had told her that a man came up behind him and struck him on the head." Interestingly, noted Thacher, these visions "all occurred within seventy-two hours of the boy's death."

Thacher spent months on the investigation, finding Rosa to be "a woman of unusual intelligence and apparently vigorous health." After conducting a series of experiments and tests, he was able to state, "There really seems to be a telepathic rapport between Mrs. Sutton and her daughters." Most significant, Thacher concluded that "Mrs. Sutton unquestionably has visions which correspond with actual happenings of which she could have no information gained in normal fashion."

Premonitions, the ability to see and hear the dead—Rosa's abilities have been known in folk culture for countless generations as "the gift." One modern-day possessor of "the gift," Mary Ann Winkowski, inherited them from her grandmother, who early on taught her to harness her powers. Winkowski has worked with law enforcement agencies and as a television consultant; her memoirs bespeak a body of experience remarkably reminiscent of Rosa Sutton's. Winkowski has cultivated a theory about "the white Light" that appears to a person at the time of death and is "the opportunity to cross over." But if the spirit fails to enter the Light, the spirit just might find itself stuck here.

"Your spirit is meant to go into the Light once it has left your body," Winkowski wrote in *When Ghosts Speak: Understanding the World of Earthbound Spirits*. "All the earthbound spirits I've spoken to . . . know that the Light is there for them and that they can walk into it. . . . [W]hen I talk to spirits who have chosen not to go into the Light, they clearly believe that their reasons for remaining earthbound are both logical and compelling."

Those who, like Jimmie Sutton, die a sudden and violent death are likely to linger, noted Winkowski. "It's not surprising when you think about it: These are the ones who most frequently choose not to go into the Light. They stay to seek justice or revenge."

And Rosa kept up the battle to clear her son's name while evidence mounted and editorials clamored for action. The *New York Times* wrote, "The fight she has made to accomplish this has, undoubtedly, been one of the bravest and most persistent battles in the modern history of motherhood."

Finally bowing to public pressure, the Navy Department resurrected the Sutton case. From July to August 1909, the Sutton Court of Inquiry held proceedings in the Naval Academy's Academic Building, now known as Mahan Hall, to reexamine the details of Sutton's death. Dr. Edward Schaeffer, former deputy coroner of Washington, D.C., and one of the most thoroughly seasoned experts alive on gunshot forensics, arrived at the court with a handgun, a human skull, and assorted other props. He painstakingly proved to all assembled that, based on the angle of the gunshot wound in Jimmie Sutton's skull, it would have been impossible for anybody except a "professional contortionist" to shoot himself in the head thusly.

To much of the public following the proceedings in detail, the suicide theory was beginning to look more and more ridiculous. But the Navy and Marine Corps remained tenacious even in the face of Dr. Schaeffer's testimony. They had held the court of inquiry the public demanded and now intended to put the matter behind them. The Suttons and those around the country who agreed with them found the court's conclusion devastatingly unsatisfying: Sutton, the court declared in the end, "was killed by a revolver shot . . . fired by himself, without the intervention of any other hand."

The expected outrage, the anticipated outcry in the press about the perceived whitewash, ensued, and still Rosa Sutton refused to give up. She may not have gotten the Navy Department to admit to anything, but enough testimony had entered the public arena to make a compelling argument that Jimmie had not committed suicide. Rosa launched a letter-writing campaign to Catholic Church officials to have her son's grave consecrated; in light of all that had come out in the court of inquiry, the Church was receptive to such a request—pending an exhumation and autopsy. And finally, nearly two years after her son's death, Rosa met with some success, for the War Department agreed to exhume Jimmie's body in Arlington National Cemetery.

The autopsy took three hours, and its conclusions were explosive. Newspaper headlines were succinct and damning: "AUTOPSY ADDS STRENGTH TO MURDER THEORY—SHOT FIRED FROM DISTANCE . . . SKULL BRUISED AND CUT, SCARS OF BATTLE CLING TO CORPSE . . . FAMILY DOCTOR SAYS SUICIDE CONTENTION IS EXPLODED."

The Navy never changed its official conclusion on the matter, but the new evidence was enough for the Roman Catholic Church. As Jimmie Sutton was laid back into the earth, a priest sprinkled holy water on the coffin and chanted in Latin. Jimmie was absolved of the sin of suicide. He now rested in holy ground. Rosa got through the prayers before she broke down.

But two things had kept Jimmie Sutton from entering the "white Light" and passing on to the eternal beyond. One was resolved with the negation of the suicide stigma and the proper burial. But the other was never resolved—for if he did not shoot himself, then someone else did, and that person or persons got away with it. Jimmie's ghost sought redemption and got it. He also sought justice and was denied it. And he still lurks at the Naval Academy today, a restive phantom angered that no one was ever punished for his murder.

Sutton's ghost has been sighted dozens of times over the years. He peeks into windows at night. He walks through walls. He wanders through buildings. Sometimes he manifests as a glowing, man-shaped mist patrolling the dark terrain where he was killed more than a century ago. In the most recently reported sighting, he was seen drifting atop the fence surrounding the Academy. Maybe he was trying to scale it, as a live young man might, to sneak out, to escape at last. But he was unable to cross to the outside. For he is bound forever to the locus of his foul and unresolved demise.

And he has company.

There is, of course, the most august company of all, the ghost of John Paul Jones heretofore chronicled. Jones' corpse was being shuffled from site to site at the Academy awaiting his crypt's completion at just the time that Sutton himself was living, and dying, there. But there are others as well; a mix of doomed hoverers from different eras imbue the grounds with a palpable aura of fearfulness on nights dark and still. A former security officer, glad to have left this particular assignment behind, remarked that "the Naval Academy at night is the scariest place I have ever been."

Perhaps some of the spirits are those of poor wretches who arrived in boatloads during the Civil War, starving and diseased, hoping to find succor in the rows of hospital tents that then lined the Academy grounds. Many were beyond saving and perished in agony. Perhaps some are those of the suicides who hanged themselves in Bancroft Hall in the 1940s and 1950s. (Across the Severn, Naval Station Annapolis is haunted by a mysterious woman in red, also said to be the evanescence of a long-forgotten suicide.)

Where so much history has unfolded, spirits are likely to linger. And the Naval Academy proves, as do so many other land quarters, that the ocean waves are not the only province of the Navy's prolific ghosts.

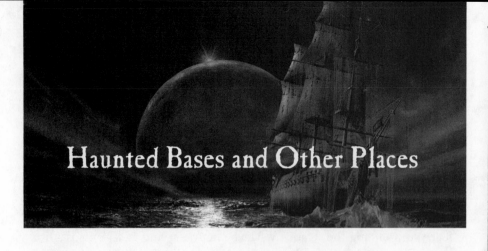

Haunted Bases and Other Places

Stephen Decatur, John Paul Jones and his fellow permanent Naval Academy denizens—they are all part of a ghostly crew that hovers and howls from coast to coast, for the haunted history of the U.S. Navy is more than just a sea-bound saga. May all lubbers therefore mark these words and accordingly beware: a spectral sailor may be encountered on land *or* sea. As an addendum to that admonition, may all sailors assigned to shore take heed as well: the fact that you are at your Navy station does not mean that the ghost you see is a fellow sailor; civilian spirits are known to invade the perimeter—or they may have been there before the Navy ever was.

A ghostly tour of America's naval landmarks begins, fittingly, with the nation's earliest significant naval yard. The officer who laid it out, oversaw its construction, and served as its first commandant remains on eternal billet at the Washington Navy Yard. In 1804, Capt. Thomas Tingey moved into the newly completed commandant's residence, Quarters A, a brick Georgian house designed (as Decatur's home would be) by architect Benjamin Henry Latrobe. Tingey, fittingly known as "the father of the Washington Navy Yard," remained at the helm through the yard's formative years and shepherded it through the crisis of 1814. When the British invaded Washington and Tingey was ordered to set fire to the yard, he was famously "the last government official to leave the city and the first to come back." Having overseen the yard's torching, he now oversaw its reconstruction. Fortunately, Quarters A had remained unharmed, and Tingey, a popular and influential figure in the social and civic life of early Washington, continued to reside there until he died in the house in 1829.

Subsequent commandants also lived in Quarters A, which came to be known as Tingey House. The house joined the National Register of Historic Places in 1973 and became the official residence of the Chief of

Naval Operations in 1979. Tingey House has changed significantly over the years, and subsequent additions have altered the original architecture. But one thing has remained constant: the presence of old Tingey. The first recorded witnessing of his ghost was in 1853, and the sightings of him since then fall into two variant patterns. He is seen either peering out the windows of the house or roaming the Navy Yard wearing a gold-braided cocked hat with a sword belted around his long flannel nightshirt and a brass spyglass under his arm. Many Quarters A residents who have not seen Tingey's specter have felt his strong presence; rather than inspiring fear, however, it is more of an encouraging entity.

In addition to being seen and felt, Captain Tingey's ghost has also been heard, quite loudly, on at least one notable occasion—the stroke of midnight on December 1, 1945, the moment when the official name of the Washington Navy Yard was changed to the U.S. Naval Gun Factory. Tingey's banshee scream was loud enough to be heard miles away. The new name did not stick, however, and the original name was reinstated in 1964; the father of the Washington Navy Yard must have been gratified.

Navy haunting grounds run the hierarchical gamut from the home of the Chief of Naval Operations to the boot camp where raw civilians are molded into sailors. Since 1911, millions of recruits have passed through the entrance of the Great Lakes Naval Training Center in Chicago, Illinois. In World War I alone the facility processed more than 100,000 trainees, and it has continued operations unabated since then in fulfillment of President Theodore Roosevelt's vision to create the world's best and largest training center. Today it comprises 1,153 buildings, 1,628 acres, and 50 miles of roadway; and some 50,000 recruits come through its gate each year. It should come as no shock that a sprawling, challenging, demanding human crossroads of this magnitude has some ectoplasm in its atmosphere.

Indeed, a bizarre and multifaceted canon of paranormal lore has accrued at Great Lakes over the years. The USO Building is haunted (incongruously) by the giggling of a little boy who augments his unsettling sounds of glee with knocking noises and swinging doors. One barracks is occupied by a ghost who can be heard doing push-ups. To those who have endured boot camp, the distinctive sound is unmistakable: the cadenced clinking of dog-tags slapping the deck, the sound of labored exhalations. It is a normal sound to hear in such environs—but not in the middle of the night, when all is still and no one is there at the source of the sound. This invisible calisthenics devotee has disturbed many a night watch. The prevailing belief is that it is the ghost of a suicide victim who hanged himself at the very spot in the 1950s, perhaps a poor soul who caved under the pressure of a pending physical training test and continues to atone in the netherworld.

A suicide-by-hanging ghost occupies another barracks as well, but his spirit is seen, not heard. Even if he were audible he might well be drowned out, for the adjacent quarters are home to a screaming ghost. No one is sure who she was in life, but in death her scream is piercing and unexpected, and then it just . . . fades away. In yet another barracks the weird and uncanny take many forms. Ghostly humanoid shapes traipse its rooms in the night—sometimes all night. Sleepers are shocked awake by a long-dead voice rasping in their ear: "Reveille! Reveille!" Once, in the presence of witnesses, a coat hanger flew off the wall, sailed across the room, and hit a sailor in the head. Stories tell that this structure was once a repository for the mentally disturbed, and that many of them perished in a fire that broke out there. Clearly, it is a spot of pronounced psychic unrest.

So, too, is Building 18. Formerly the base hospital, it was the site of more than one hundred deaths—and now is home to multiple hauntings. In addition to patients who died of illness or injury, the presences here include a nurse who killed herself by plunging from a high window. She still revisits the building and even has spoken to the living. An unidentified officer sometimes speaks to current occupants who, with mounting horror, realize that while he is clear and visibly outlined, the man speaking to them is semitransparent, like a hologram that grows more garbled and blurred before fading away.

Less charmingly loquacious are the foreboding spirits of Quarters A, where a maid died under mysterious circumstances. Was it suicide—or murder? Either way, her untimely departure would seem to account for the recurrent sightings of a woman in white on the top deck. But what to make of the disturbing visions of an admiral's son who once lived in Quarters A and told his parents that he had seen "Satan" in his bedroom? The evil, hulking thing that threatened the boy certainly did not match the description of the maid's ghost. Nor was there anything specifically suggestive of armed-forces personnel, such as a uniform or general deportment might indicate. Could the "Satan" of Quarters A be older than Quarters A itself?

Some of the inexplicable phenomena that abound at Great Lakes may indeed predate the Navy's presence. Archaeologists have discovered that the training center was built atop an old frontier cemetery. The graves of irascible, diehard pioneers have been disturbed, and to what consequence? Some investigators theorize that the "Satan" seen by the admiral's son was the ghost of a wild frontiersman. The mystery of the giggling child in the USO Building might also be explained by the preexisting presence of the pioneer dead. No families ever resided in the building, but the impish laughter could be that of a settler's child who, as so many did in the old days, died very young.

The Great Lakes Naval Training Center's mixed bag of ghosts is in keeping with the situation at other stations around the country where sailors must commingle with the restless shades of the past. The U.S. Naval Postgraduate School, housed in the stucco grandeur of the former Hotel Del Monte in Monterey, California, is haunted by various enigmatic wraiths, clingers-on never able to check out of the luxurious venue. Like so many majestic old hotels, it is rife with mysterious occurrences and unnerving indications of a dimension not of the living. The pall of creepiness is compounded by the fact that the Del Monte is the *third* hotel of the same name to occupy the site since the 1870s; and the first two ended catastrophically, each in a roar of all-consuming flames. Among the ghosts who stalk the dark corners of the Naval Postgraduate School is one believed to be the fire chief who was unable to save the original hotel when it burned in 1887. Another frequently appearing ghost, a wandering man in an old-fashioned gray suit, is hypothesized to be Charles Crocker, a tycoon who helped bankroll the original hotel's construction.

Naval personnel haunted by preexisting presences: such was the case back in Washington, D.C., at Tracy House, which before the ghastly events of 1890 stood tall and stately off Connecticut Avenue in the vicinity of Lafayette Square. Benjamin Franklin Tracy, secretary of the Navy during the administration of President Benjamin Harrison, refused to heed warnings that the attractive house was a place of evil. For nearly twenty years, tales had been told of a brutal murder there, tales of a lady in white roaming throughout the house, plaintively and repeatedly uttering an indecipherable word—a name, perhaps? So frequently did the sad ghost promenade through the house that it was nearly impossible to maintain tenants in the cursed dwelling.

A tailor and his new bride had taken up residence there in the 1870s. Neighbors soon noticed that the tailor always seemed to emerge from the house alone and routinely evaded questions about his wife. After the tailor moved out, subsequent residents complained of tapping in the walls,

of blood-curdling moans. The house eventually came into the hands of
a man determined to restore and renovate it. As he took down a wall, he
discovered a skeleton. A wedding ring still hung loosely on a finger bone,
and a silver letter opener encrusted with desiccated blood dangled from
the ribcage. From that point on, the lady in white—the tailor's slain
bride—prowled from room to room, filling the air with her mournful,
garbled entreaties.

But Secretary Tracy would have none of such drivel. Intending to stay
there for the tenure of his appointment, he and his family moved into
the house. But not for long: shortly after the Tracys took up residence, an
unexplained fire broke out and utterly destroyed the place with shocking
rapidity. Secretary Tracy's wife and daughter were killed in the conflagration—and then new tales were told, of a restless energy liberated at last
from the never-ending and fruitless room-by-room quest for her fickle and
homicidal groom.

A pathetic, lovelorn spirit likewise hovers over the Charleston Naval
Base in South Carolina. Its resident ghost is that of a woman who is spied
in the trees along the riverbank, where she waits forever for the Englishman
who promised to help her escape from slavery. In payment for his assistance she brought him the mistress' jewels. The faithless Englishman took
the jewels, shoved her to the ground, and left without her. Brokenhearted,
and now facing dire punishment for having pilfered the jewelry, the young
woman returned to the manor and burned it to the ground, concealing
her offense by the most epic possible means. That was in 1796. Today, at
the Charleston Naval Base, few vestiges remain of that perfidious night of
southern Gothic tragedy—save for a sad wraith with futile patience lurking on the river's edge.

Two states north of South Carolina, at the U.S. Naval Weapons
Station near Yorktown, Virginia, further echoes of tragedy from the past
bedevil sailors of the present. Imagine what it must be like for those on
watch along the base perimeter when, out of the blackness, the piercing screams of women and the panicked neighing of horses shatter the
midnight silence. Shouts are raised, lights flash and search—but there are
no women, no horses. It is just the latest supernatural reenactment of a
fatal mishap of the late seventeenth century. The daughter of Governor
Edward Digges of Virginia was rolling homeward with her friends on the
Old Williamsburg Road after an evening's festivities in Yorktown when
the driver lost his bearings in the darkness and the carriage careened into

the Black Swamp. It took mere moments for the evil mud to ingest the screaming young ladies, the desperate and wild-eyed horses, the luckless carriage. In the dead of night, the dead still rise from this foul morass to suffer anew their final moments of terror.

The nearby U.S. Naval Shipyard at Norfolk, Virginia, likewise plays host to old guests who can never leave. This sprawling and venerable complex, whose first dry dock was constructed in 1767, includes numerous buildings that incorporate timbers from old sailing ships. Wood pragmatically recycled for construction purposes can also carry with it the transposed spirits of those long-forgotten vessels. Can it be coincidental that Buildings 29, 31, and 33—all of which have remnants of the age of sail in their bones—are the principal haunts of the shipyard's most high-profile ghost? He has long been known among yard personnel by the nickname "John Paul," a nod to his eighteenth-century attire suggestive of John Paul Jones. John Paul is an oft-appearing and vivid phantom—so vivid, in fact, that a sailor in 1918 experienced raw panic at the sight of him, and in his frantic efforts to escape from the ghost broke a leg.

John Paul is not alone on the spectral plane at the Norfolk yard. There is the compulsively tidy ghost of Quarters B fussily moving mishung keys onto their proper pegs on the key rack by the door. There are the floating white blobs and flickering lights of the former sailmaking loft, where eerie voices and the rat-a-tat of long-gone sewing machines chatter on through time. There is the trio of British soldiers from the Revolutionary War or War of 1812 whose long-forgotten graves were disturbed in 1971, and who now haunt Dry Docks 1 and 2.

A ghost of more recent vintage occupies the mess hall at nearby Naval Air Station Norfolk. During the Korean War, a sailor was murdered while lunching here. Although there were witnesses to the event, all kept mum. The mess hall ghost is an angry presence. If he is summoned by name, objects will move through the air, propelled by an unseen hand.

The Navy's land-bound ghosts hail from many eras and range in temperament from benign to forlorn to malevolent. They manifest in differing degrees of clarity, from walking, talking exact replicas of their original selves to weird clouds of floating energy. But in all that spectral parade, none is more entrancing, more alluring than the mysterious nude ghost of Dam Neck Naval Base in Virginia Beach. She appeared just before dawn on a cold December morning in 1999 in the women's-wing showers. A sailor was showering before going on leave when she witnessed the sudden and physics-defying entrance of "a transparent naked slender woman with dark black straight hair." The ghostly Godiva came right through a wall and proceeded on her way, seemingly impervious to her shivering witness. Where did she come from? Where was she going? Above all, who *was* she? She will remain an intriguing enigma until all the facts can be laid bare.

Sometimes ghost identification is much simpler—especially when a haunted house bears the name of the ghost who haunts it. Case in point: Lynch Hall, the handsome (albeit spooky-looking) Tudor mansion that serves as the administrative nerve center of the University of Pittsburgh at Greensburg. Before assuming its academic role the building was the home of Cdr. Charles McKenna Lynch, USN, who built the house in 1923 and named it Starboard Light. Commander Lynch, a veteran of both world wars, died in the house in 1963. The University of Pittsburgh acquired the property from the Lynch family the following year and established a branch campus. Starboard Light became Lynch Hall, the new school's first facility. A twenty-three-building institute of higher learning grew up around it. And the generations of students who have attended the University of Pittsburgh at Greensburg have come to accept "the ghost of Commander Lynch" as a facet of campus life.

Sightings have been frequent through the years; one person who worked in Lynch Hall even reported seeing the commander wearing full-dress Navy uniform. Psychics brought in to investigate the house have been bowled over by the powerful aura. The emanations radiate most strongly from the area where Commander Lynch's office used to be and a spiral staircase winds upward to second-floor living quarters. One night a security officer who had entered the bathroom in this section to shut and lock the window sensed movement on her periphery. In the tub. She turned slowly. A wizened man with eyes sunk deep in their sockets was sitting in the tub with his legs drawn close to his chest. He stared at her wordlessly, though her mind heard him asking why she had intruded on him. She turned away. She looked again. He was still there, still staring at her. She fled, returning with another officer. The tub was empty.

Commander Lynch also has been seen clad in retro-looking civilian attire leaning on the banister at the top of the stairs. He has been heard, too, even when not seen. "Once I was in here alone and I heard the back door open and keys jingling," another security officer recalled. "It startled me and when I walked back that way there was no one there. . . . I mean, there are noises in this house like the pipes when the boilers kick on, but that one I can't explain, especially the keys jingling." According to psychics the entity here is not a threatening one; even the bathroom incident, though harrowing, was more a case of privacy's basic territorialism. If anything, the ghost is rather good-natured (with perhaps a sense of mischief); the commander simply still likes to make the rounds.

Less jocular, evidently, is the spirit that occupies the former home of Rear Adm. J. H. Hawley in Whitefield, New Hampshire. Admiral Hawley in the early 1900s was a part of the Washington, D.C., elite that made the fashionable annual summer pilgrimage to New Hampshire's White Mountains. Admiral and Mrs. Hawley went from staying at guesthouses to building their own summer Shangri-La in the Edenic New England woods. The admiral named the three-story white house with wraparound porch Mizzentop. After his retirement, the Hawleys made Mizzentop their full-time residence. Admiral Hawley died there in 1925. Subsequent owners of the property began to speak ill of him when they discovered that the house came fully equipped with a dour and malicious energy.

The admiral's daughter sold the property to a couple who renovated the attic to create a playroom for their son and his friends. They cut new windows in the walls and disposed of the Hawleys' possessions that had remained in storage, all but forgotten, in the dusty attic. It was when they tossed out the admiral's sea chest that the troubles began.

First there were the footsteps—footsteps in the attic, footsteps on the stairs to the attic, footsteps in the hallway leading to the stairs. Then there was the sound of heavy breathing and the dragging, groaning noise of objects being moved in the attic, in the hall. Then came the tormenting of the psychically sensitive maid, whose bed was shaken violently as if by invisible hands on the posts, so violently that she evacuated it in panic; as soon as she got out of the bed, the rocking stopped.

By 1965, when Mizzentop was examined by renowned paranormalist Hans Holzer with his frequent investigative partner, the psychic Sybil Leek (the same pair who conducted the seminal USS *Constellation* ghost search), the property was in the possession of the man whose parents had purchased the property from the Hawley family. The man had spent his childhood there—the attic playroom from Hell had been fashioned with him in mind—and now he and his wife and their young son used the house as a summer home. But even such limited use had become paranormally problematic. The owner had more recent phenomena to report to Holzer and Leek. Ten years earlier, he and his new bride had honeymooned here, only to have the occasion dampened by "a general feeling of eeriness and a feeling that there was someone else in the house. There were footsteps in the hall outside our bedroom door. At one point before dawn, the steps went up the stairs and walked around overhead." They checked, of course. And no one else was in the house.

Chilling though the experience was, the stalwart pair nonetheless continued to return periodically to the house in the woods. Four years before Holzer and Leek came to investigate the Mizzentop phenomena, the owner had gone up to the attic to grab a book, "when suddenly I walked into what I can only describe as a *warm, wet blanket*, something that touched me physically as if it had been hung by wires in the corridor."

He retreated quickly. When he got back downstairs, his astounded wife remarked that he looked white as a sheet.

"I know," he said. "I think I just walked into the admiral."

And there had been other recent incidents. The couple's young son had been awakened by a voice—a man's voice, unrecognizable, speaking the boy's name. A visiting friend watched the attic doorknob turn by itself, and his suddenly distraught dog refused to go in there. The owner's wife watched the kitchen door open and close by itself, soon to be followed by the front door opening and closing by itself.

Once on site, Holzer and Leek got to work. While Holzer recorded interviews, Leek explored the nooks and crannies of the ghost house in search of psychic power spots. She homed in on the second-floor room where Admiral Hawley had died. "There is a man lying dead in the middle room," she intoned from her trance. She ended up in the attic, where she made direct contact with the spirit. The connection was full of static, but she identified the presence as Hawley. He was angry about the changes made to his house, angry about his displaced possessions, angry as well about what he viewed as a general air of untidiness.

No subsequent paranormal investigations have been permitted at the property. The house remains in private hands, and the status of its haunting remains a private matter. Do Admiral Hawley's ghostly footfalls still descend the nocturnal hallways of Mizzentop? One thing is clear: if an admiral wants things shipshape and Bristol fashion, it is advisable to make them so.

Another admiral—the Navy's first, in fact, and one of its greatest—also has taken up ghostly residence in New Hampshire. David Glasgow Farragut—the naval hero of the Civil War, the victor of the Battle of

Mobile Bay, the officer hailed as "the Union's Nelson"—can now be found peacefully seated in a leather chair by the fireplace in Quarters A at the Portsmouth Naval Shipyard.

Ironically, the storied admiral never was actually stationed at this storied yard. But it was fated to be his final resting place at the end of one of naval history's most illustrious careers. Born in 1801, the son of a Spanish sailor who fought for his adopted land in the Revolution and the War of 1812, David Glasgow Farragut joined the Navy at an early age, rising through the ranks until the man and the moment were met in the Civil War. Commanding the Western Gulf Blockading Squadron, he led his wooden fleet up the Mississippi in April 1862, defied all prevailing military wisdom by successfully making it past the fort defenses of New Orleans, and launched the battle that led to the city's capitulation. Great as this victory was, Farragut's ultimate hour of glory came on August 5, 1864, when, lashed high in the rigging of his flagship, he uttered his bold and immortal command, "Damn the torpedoes! Full speed ahead!" and further cracked open the Mississippi for the Union in the Battle of Mobile Bay. A grateful President Abraham Lincoln created the rank of vice admiral in order to be able to promote Farragut to it. Commissioning as full admiral soon followed by an act of Congress in 1866; Farragut thus became the first officer in the U.S. Navy to hold the rank.

On August 14, 1870, Admiral Farragut was visiting his brother-in-law, Commo. A. M. Pennock, commander of the Portsmouth Naval Shipyard. The sixty-nine-year-old admiral had been in poor health since his Mississippi campaigns, and had recently suffered a heart attack. He had had a premonition of impending death, which took him while he was visiting his brother-in-law in residence at Quarters A, Portsmouth.

And so this stately old house surrounded by modern shipyard sprawl became the final home of one of the Navy's finest. If one is to have a ghost tenant, the admiral would be one to welcome. "For our two years in residence, we felt the admiral's ghost 'looking after things' in Quarters A," recalled a shipyard commander's wife in her memoir of 1950s life in the house. "He was there, constantly on alert, as one after another of the Navy families came and went through the years."

At one point the admiral's ghost reportedly tipped over a glass of champagne during a speech. He has also been known to close shutters during the day. Sometimes he has been ignominiously reduced to the role of scapegoat. A shipyard commander of the 1970s remembered with bemusement, "My kids, when I asked them about it, whenever some liquor was missing, they always said, 'Admiral Farragut took it.'"

The admiral's main haunt is by the fireplace, right where he died and where a seat is kept for him. But he has also been seen or felt near the back stairway. A former resident remembers how her children used to run up and down those stairs, and how they were particularly attuned to the admiral's presence, almost as if they were playing with him on the stairs. "They felt it very definitely, and felt he was very much in charge. He was just there. It was not frightening to them. We just all felt he was right there, looking after things."

How comforting to think that those who embodied the spirit of the Navy and are now themselves spirits, in some sense are still right here, looking after things.

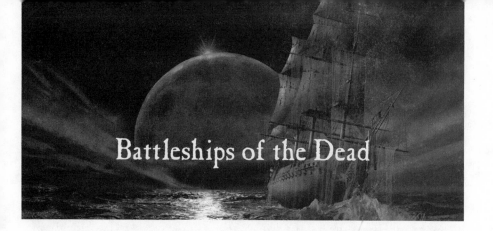

Battleships of the Dead

David Glasgow Farragut sailed to victory with a wooden fleet at the Battle of New Orleans in 1862. Two years later, at the Battle of Mobile Bay, his squadron also included a quartet of strange, new-fangled-looking monstrosities: ironclad monitors. America's first admiral thus straddled the cusp of the ages of sail and steam, of wood and steel. The century that had begun with the age of fighting sail at its zenith would conclude with world powers trapped in an escalating contest to see which could build the biggest, most indomitable metallic behemoths of the sea. The dawn of the nineteenth century had seen Nelson at Trafalgar; the dawn of the twentieth saw the eve of the mighty dreadnought era. HMS *Dreadnought*, launched in 1906, gave her name to both the new age and the new supercraft that ruled it. The lumbering, thick-skinned giants bristling with big-gun firepower rendered obsolete all preexisting warships afloat. Empires old and new joined in the dreadnought construction boom, and for decades the great ships ruled the waves and defined sea power. Only one of them remains. She is American, and she is haunted.

When she rolled off the ways on May 18, 1912, no one knew, of course, that the USS *Texas* would someday hold the distinction of being "The Last of the Dreadnoughts," as she has come to be fondly nicknamed. What they did know was that the *Texas* was the mightiest ship of her day, the dreadnought of all dreadnoughts—27,000 tons and 573 feet from stem to stern. Her arsenal included ten 14-inch guns mounted in pairs in five turrets; they were the largest guns in the world at the time, and she was the first ship to have them. A battleship of the *New York* class, the *Texas* was destined for a long and action-packed career, including laudatory service in two world wars. From 1914, when she was officially commissioned, until 1948, when she was finally retired, the *Texas* logged 728,000 miles from Iceland to South America, from the Mediterranean to the Pacific, and crossed the Panama Canal sixteen times. In her thirty-four years and six weeks of naval service (only the *Arkansas* topped the *Texas* in longevity of commission), the *Texas* underwent seventeen gun reconfigurations and witnessed the switch from coal to fuel and the introduction of electronics. She sailed across the crucial first half of the American Century, ever adapting, ever active. She was the first U.S. Navy ship to have an aircraft launched from her deck (March 9, 1919) and the first to have radar installed. Hers was the first ship launching filmed by a motion picture camera, and she is the last surviving warship in the world to have fought in both world wars. And somewhere along the way, at some spot in her forays into harm's way around the globe, the *Texas* picked up a ghostly occupant. Who is this enigmatic sailor specter who over the years has come to be known as "Red"? Red himself is not telling. He simply stands there, looks you in the eye, and smiles a beaming yet inscrutable smile. And then he is gone.

He *did* speak—once—to save a man's life. And he has generated nonverbal noises in order to convey dire warnings. But the majority of his manifestations have been strictly visual phenomena accented by neither whispers nor screams; only that mute and mysterious grin. Did he die on board or did he return to his favorite berth in life after dying elsewhere? He seems, above all, a protective spirit. From what chapter of the battleship's illustrious saga does he spring?

If Red is one of the original crew of the *Texas*, then he was part of a complement of 1,072 officers and men who first sailed her into action at Veracruz in May 1914. They were providing support to the U.S. troops landing in retaliation for the Tampico incident, in which Mexican troops had detained U.S. sailors, sparking a tense international situation. It was the warm-up for a conflict of a more global nature. The *Texas* served in World War I as part of the American Battleship Division, a valued auxiliary to Great Britain's Grand Fleet, helping to keep Germany's High Seas Fleet bottled up in port and providing protection to minelayers putting down the massive North Sea mine belt that stretched from Scotland to Norway. After the war, the *Texas* spent the 1920s and 1930s intermittently fulfilling the role of flagship of the U.S. fleet, conveying President Calvin Coolidge to the Pan-American Conference in Havana in 1928, escorting the ship carrying the American delegation home from the London Naval Conference in 1930, alternating between Atlantic and Pacific duties. In late 1939, after the outbreak of World War II in Europe, the *Texas* was on patrol in the North Atlantic, drilling for battle when not patrolling, preparing for the inevitable.

The inevitable came on December 7, 1941, borne on the wings of Japanese bombers, and the United States entered the fray. The *Texas* alternated between convoy missions and combat, embarking in October 1942 as flagship of the attack group carrying out Operation Torch, the invasion of North Africa. She maneuvered along the coast of Morocco, unleashing ship-to-shore barrages in support of the Army assault force. From June 6–18, 1944, she lent her firepower to the Normandy invasion as flagship of the Omaha Beach bombardment group, blasting German emplacements; taking out snipers, machine-gun nests, and mortars; then bombarding antiaircraft batteries and German troops farther inland. She fought off a night attack by a German plane on her starboard quarter and kept raining 14-inch shells down on the foe's fortified inland positions until the action had moved east beyond her range.

But the guns of the *Texas* would not have much time to cool down. June 25 found her hotly engaged in the battle for Cherbourg; joined by the battleship *Arkansas*, the *Texas* unloaded round upon round on the German fortifications and batteries ringing the French port city. The Germans were quick to fire back. Thick spumes of angry water gushed skyward to port and starboard as the *Texas* wove through enemy near-misses and continued her shore bombardment. A German 280-millimeter shell finally found its mark, and the fire control tower exploded. The helmsman was killed and virtually everyone else on the navigation bridge was wounded. Another German shell, a 240-millimeter armor-piercer, smashed through the port bow and landed below the wardroom before fizzling. Through it all, through the smoke and destruction and casualties, the *Texas* kept up her fire, retiring only when ordered after three hours of heavy fighting. Next up for her was the Mediterranean, and shore bombardment duties in support of the August invasion of southern France. The Axis shell was cracking, and World War II already had availed the tough old battlewagon of enough sea stories to last her well into retirement. But for the *Texas*, as for the Navy, this was to be a two-ocean war.

She had been there for Operation Torch and D-day—the hinges on which the war in the West had swung, and now the *Texas* would participate in the momentous final act in the Pacific Theater as well. Through the last two weeks of February 1945 she relentlessly pummeled the deeply entrenched Japanese defenses on Iwo Jima, first in preparation for the storm landings, then offering directed support fire for the Marines as they carried out their arduous and bloody mission to conquer the island, crucial stepping-stone to the home islands of Japan. The fortnight off Iwo was the most intensive period yet for the gunnery crews of the *Texas*, who pounded the indefatigable Japanese defenders with nearly two thousand rounds of 14-inch and 5-inch shells. But this level of intensity was about to be topped, even doubled.

If Iwo Jima was one of the war's signature epics—replete with struggle, death, heroism, and tragedy in outsized portions—Okinawa was the crucible of victory in the Pacific. If Iwo Jima had demonstrated that the closer American forces got to Japan, the more determinedly the Japanese troops stood their ground, then Okinawa, their last stand, illustrated what desperate men with nothing to lose could do. For six days starting on March 26, the *Texas* hurled salvo after punishing salvo of 14-inch shellfire, a ruthless daily bombardment in preparation for the pending landing of Army and Marine Corps troops. They stormed onto the sand on April 1, and the long fight was on. For nearly two months the *Texas* kept up her heavy fire, all the while fending off kamikaze attacks, including one suicide plane that sheared off a wing and crashed onto the starboard bow. When it was all over, when the Byzantine subterranean mazes all had been cleared, when the never-say-die samurai spirit of the Japanese troops finally yielded to the inexorable tide of the massed onslaught, the *Texas* had all but melted her guns to their turrets, expending more than 2,000 14-inch rounds, more than 2,600 5-inch rounds, and several thousand antiaircraft rounds as well.

The worldwide cataclysm was coming to a close, and none who fought their way through it would ever be the same. August 15, 1945—V-J Day— found the *Texas* off Okinawa in Bruckner Bay. After all she had endured, after all she had been both witness and party to in both hemispheres of the war, her final assignment was one of hope, of deliverance from the horrors. As part of Operation Magic Carpet, the *Texas* transported 4,267 American troops back home from the Pacific in time for Christmas 1945.

It was a poignant capstone to a remarkable career. In 1948 the *Texas* arrived at San Jacinto State Park near Houston; her eponymous state would be her permanent home, and the site commemorating the early heroes of the war for Texas independence would be her anchorage of honor. Struck from the Navy List in April of that year, the *Texas* became the first Navy ship to be transferred by act of Congress to museum status, the first such floating memorial; there are more now, but still, sadly, precious few.

Workers restoring the ship soon reported strange goings-on. A sailor in what looked to be an old-style uniform appeared before a workman and warned him to clear the deck quickly. Had he not heeded the ghostly admonishment, the laborer would have been rendered unconscious within moments by toxic paint fumes that would certainly have killed the helpless man. A welder was next to be saved, his efforts repeatedly interrupted by a loud tapping. Every time he started to fire up his blowtorch, the insistent tapping would start again. He went below to find the source of the noise but saw and heard nothing. Closer investigation with a flashlight revealed containers leaking fuel; his torch, once lit, would have triggered an explosion. The disaster was avoided thanks to the anonymous tapper.

Mostly, though, the ghost simply appears. His nickname, Red, refers to his bright hair. He is most often seen standing alongside a ladder on Deck 2 wearing a white sailor's uniform and a big smile. Once, multiple witnesses tried to chase him down, to no avail. Red doesn't always appear as his usual vivid, well-detailed self; one group of visitors on the ship saw a vaguely defined, cloudy mass moving along a passageway. Are the cloud figure and the tapping lifesaver also manifestations of Red or different spirits entirely?

If all of them are Red, and he is in fact the *Texas*'s sole spirit, then he may well be the ghost of the helmsman killed in the fire control tower explosion during the Battle of Cherbourg in 1944. His was, amazingly, the only death on board the *Texas* during her service, though there were numerous casualties. But one need only recall the *Constellation*, and the presence thereon of the ghost of Capt. Thomas Truxtun, who died on land but chose to return to his old ship. It is not unheard-of for the ghost of a longtime seafarer to seek the lilt of a good deck beneath his feet rather than wallow in limbo on land.

And there may be more supernatural mysteries on the *Texas* than an affable red-haired ghost. There is something weird about the trophy room, also on Deck 2. To those innately attuned to occult vibrations, it seems to be some sort of portal. A caretaker swore that she entered the trophy room and was sucked into a warp in the space-time continuum. She was transported to a far-off sea—a sea of gravestones, that is, in a military cemetery in Normandy.

The bizarre reports emanating from the Last of the Dreadnoughts finally spurred the Texas-based paranormal detection team Lone Star Spirits to launch an investigation in 1998. The sight of ghost hunters with armloads of audiovisual scanning equipment ascending the gangplank no doubt caused the smiling sailor to shy away into the shadows, for it seems to be the nature of ghosts to appear when they are not expected and to lay low when hunted. But the ghost of the *Texas* could not keep his presence entirely hidden from the Lone Star Spirits. Their probe yielded a significant electromagnetic field (EMF) spike and a photograph capturing an inexplicable patch of light. If it didn't make the investigators sound as if they were angry, you might say . . . they saw Red.

* * *

While paranormalist scrutiny will continue to focus on the mysteries of the *Texas*, she is not the only battleship to harbor the ghostly remnants of a martial past. The USS *North Carolina*, a veteran of some of the fiercest action of the war in the Pacific, is home to a gallimaufry of spirits, and not all of them are as blithe as the smiling, protective *Texas* phantom. In some dim quarters of this vast floating tomb malevolence can be felt, a dark pall of dread, reverberations of some past terror.

Just as the *Texas*, in terms of battleship architecture, is the last of the old breed, the *North Carolina* is the first of the new. Laid down in 1937, launched in 1940, and commissioned in 1941, the *North Carolina* aroused widespread interest among the American public from the very beginning. She was the first of the Navy's modern battleships, the first U.S. battleship commissioned since 1923. (The 1922 Washington Naval Treaty had put an international moratorium on the construction of capital ships. No more arms races, no more world wars. That hope was dead by 1940.) Here was a brave new battleship indeed: 35,000 tons, nearly 729 feet long, her abundant armaments including nine 16-inch guns with more punch and accuracy than any that had come before. She drew such rapturous attention during her fitting out and shakedown that she earned a nickname, "Showboat," that has stuck with her to this day.

But it would soon be abundantly evident that she was no mere show pony. From late 1942 through 1945 the *North Carolina* slugged it out in one major Pacific engagement after another. At the Battle of the Eastern Solomons (August 23–25, 1942) her gunners shot down at least seven and perhaps as many as fourteen Japanese planes within one eight-minute stretch while bombs dropped all around them. While the ship remained largely unscathed, Japanese strafing did kill a *North Carolina* crewman.

On September 6, while supporting the Marines on Guadalcanal, the *North Carolina* pulled off an adroit maneuver and dodged a torpedo from a Japanese submarine. But she wasn't so lucky on the fifteenth, when a Japanese torpedo smashed through the *North Carolina*'s port side twenty feet below the waterline, killing five men. The battleship was listing, but the well-trained crew soon succeeded in righting the doughty vessel.

After repairs she continued the hard slog of island-hopping across the Pacific, protecting aircraft carriers, supporting troops on shore, downing enemy aircraft, destroying enemy island defenses, sinking enemy vessels. The Gilberts and the Marshall Islands. Saipan. The Philippine Sea. Leyte. Iwo Jima. Okinawa. Tokyo Bay. The *North Carolina* rumbled through the bloodiest seas to the bitter end. She earned her battle scars, one of which was particularly unfortunate: on April 6, 1945, during the bombardment of Okinawa, the *North Carolina* succeeded in splashing three kamikaze planes but was hit by friendly fire, a wayward 5-inch shell hurled out amid the massive multiship fireworks display of antiaircraft fire. Forty-four *North Carolina* crewmen were wounded and three were killed. They were the last to die aboard her.

After the war, the battleship remained in reserve after she was decommissioned in 1947. Struck from the Navy List in 1960, she had been fated for the scrap yard but was rescued by a vigorous "Save Our Ship" campaign launched by the people of North Carolina. She was transferred over to that state in 1961 and is today a popular attraction in Wilmington. And as her proud tower stands its perennial watch on the Cape Fear River, restive spirits—some merely prankish, others threateningly angry—lurk in the shadows, creep in the passageways, stare menacingly through portholes, hover at hatchways, and scream.

In 1976 the *North Carolina*'s live-aboard caretaker decided he'd had enough and was ready to pass on the job to someone else, someone who could handle the long, lonely nights on the haunted battleship. "Shoot, I can sleep through anything," avowed Danny Bradshaw when his predecessor warned him what to expect. The workload was relatively minor, the responsibilities were finite, and the degree of solitude was desirable to a person so inclined, as Bradshaw was. Save for the admonition about ghosts on board, the job was too good to be true.

Bradshaw soon discovered that any dream job has a catch to it, and in this case the catch was just as advertised—a superfluity of the supernatural. Venturing below one night to a storage area to grab an extra side table for

his quarters, he felt an overwhelming sense of foreboding, then jumped
in shock when a sudden sharp voice, a voice without a body, screamed,
"Get out!" Bradshaw promptly did just that. It turned out that the storage
area was near the spot where the Japanese torpedo struck in 1942, killing
five sailors. The hatch leading down to this part of the ship displayed a
tendency to slam shut by itself—a four-inch-thick iron hatch weighing
approximately five hundred pounds, angled back so it was impossible for
it to close accidentally, and held in place by a sturdy hook. The hook had
been released and the mighty hatch shoved closed, yet there was no one
else on board.

Then there was the night that Bradshaw was in the middle of a phone
call when he heard an unmistakable sound. Someone was crumpling paper.
He turned around to see, with horror, two sheets of paper being balled up,
suspended in midair by an invisible hand. A deathly chill filled the room.
Bradshaw high-tailed it to the parking lot and spent the rest of the night
in his car.

That cold gust, a vile and depressing miasma like the breath of doom
itself, was a recurring phenomenon. One night a friend came aboard to
play cards with Bradshaw. The Carolina air was pleasantly cool that evening, and there was no need to have air conditioners or fans running on
the battleship. The poker game was proceeding enjoyably when a heavy
sensation of profound dread engulfed the room. That was soon followed by
a shocking wave of Arctic air. "Danny, there is something very evil in this
room," his friend gasped, rising so quickly that he knocked over his chair.
"Let's get the hell out of here!"

Bradshaw by now knew that the ghosts, his fellow occupants of the
ship, came and went at will. Though consumed by fear as well, he struggled
to maintain his composure and tried to calm his friend. But his friend was
by now entering the realm of sheer panic.

"The cold air is all over me." His voice was shaking. "I can't take this
any longer, Danny, it's freaking me out!"

The death chill passed and the temperature instantly normalized. But
a relaxing game of poker was no longer in the cards. Danny walked his
friend down to the parking lot. "That was the scariest feeling I ever had in
my life," the friend said, then drove away without even waving good-bye.
He didn't come back for a long time.

The *North Carolina* tended to have that effect on Bradshaw's visitors.
A friend called one evening to announce that she had prepared a home-

cooked fried-chicken dinner for him—manna from Heaven to a ship-bound bachelor. He went down to the parking lot to help carry aboard the feast. She had just pulled in and was farther down the lot, alongside the section of the ship where his quarters were. She was honking her horn. When he walked over to her, she asked, "Who's your company?"

He didn't know what she meant.

She said, "Someone is in your room."

She had seen a face in the porthole. She had thought it was Danny and had honked to get him to come down and help her.

His room was padlocked shut. There was no one else on board.

Tensely, with mounting fear, they turned to look at the porthole to Bradshaw's quarters.

A face was staring back at them. After a moment it turned away and the curtain was closed.

Bradshaw's friend screamed. He had no explanation for her. She drove off in a terrified hurry without even dropping off his hot dinner. He gathered his courage and cautiously approached the door to his quarters. It was still padlocked shut, just as he had left it. He went in. All was as it should be. No one was there. "There was no way for anybody to get in or out of that room," he insisted in his memoir. So, who, or what, had they seen at the porthole? It wasn't just hunger pangs that kept Bradshaw wide awake that night.

There was even an occasion where a spirit resident of the battleship attempted to reenact an earthly pleasure loved by sailors everywhere: shore leave. Bradshaw's girlfriend at the time swung by in her van before heading out to a party; shipboard duties precluded him from joining her, so she came around for a quick hello. After promising to call him later, she headed off. She was barely out of the parking lot when the coldness gripped her. "I have never felt such a strange cold in my life. The further I drove the worse it got." Within minutes, objects in the rear of the van started flying around, banging and caroming off the sides, everything back there—from books to a beach chair to snaking jumper cables—suddenly, violently airborne. Screaming hysterically, she screeched into the nearest gas station where a gentleman offered his assistance. She told him someone was in the back of her van. He searched it for her. There was nobody there.

Distraught, she returned to the *North Carolina* where Bradshaw tried to calm her nerves. As she left the parking lot for a second time she noticed "the funniest thing. . . . The temperature in the van went back to normal and that eerie feeling left."

Her van's haunting was blessedly temporary, a ghost on loan. Back on board the *North Carolina*, the spectral activity remains rampant and unpredictable. Of all her forever crew, the most frightening is the "blond" ghost who first appeared to Bradshaw belowdecks one night as he was flipping off power switches. The ship had been cleared of tourists, and his flashlight illuminated the power box as he went through his nightly routine. When he felt a hand on his shoulder, Bradshaw was overwhelmed by knee-buckling fear. It wasn't just that no one else was on board. The hand on his shoulder was accompanied by the terrifying Arctic cold.

He forced himself to turn around. His flashlight beam illumined an empty passageway although footsteps clicked nearby. And then, where there had been empty space, a man now stood, glaring with intense anger. His swirling hair was so blond as to be bright white. The flashlight beam cut right through him.

At Bradshaw's guttural and involuntary scream the entity turned away and vanished. Bradshaw ran for his life. As he flew up the ladder he was stopped by the sound of footsteps, those same footsteps from a minute ago but above him now, descending the same ladder. All he could think was, "Please, God, let me out. I don't want to die here." He slid back down the ladder and ran forward to another exit, clambered out, and didn't stop moving until he was off the ship and in his car. "It was the horriblest thing I've ever experienced," he told a reporter. Unfortunately, he was destined to run into the same ghost again. And what he thought had been white blond hair, he came to realize, was actually *flames*.

And the litany of oddities continued to grow: weird running footsteps, doorknobs turning by themselves, a shower spigot turning by itself, a television turning off by itself, a moving-chair incident that sent a group of tourists packing in abject terror. It was inevitable that the *North Carolina* would come to the attention of ghost investigators. Several waves of paranormal research teams have peered into the multitudinous nooks and crannies of the mammoth battleship. Seven Paranormal Research, an organization dedicated to exploring the bizarre and strange throughout North Carolina, endeavored to set up an overnight stakeout with three strategically placed cameras. For reasons unexplained, all three cameras simultaneously switched off at 9:35 PM. All three had fully charged batteries, and all three died at the same moment. Coincidence? Professor Al Profitt of Western Carolina University, author of works on regional paranormal phenomena, spent the night on the *North Carolina* and reported hearing disembodied footsteps and objects moving about. Exploring the area below the waterline where the torpedo had struck, his freshly charged flashlight suddenly quit working. When he returned topside, the flashlight shone brightly again.

When the famous Atlantic Paranormal Society (TAPS) team arrived in 2005 to study the battleship for their television program, *Ghost Hunters*, they joined forces with the local group Haunted North Carolina for two nights of intensive ship scrutiny. The results were compelling: dramatic EMF fluctuations, wildly dropping temperatures, a self-shutting hatch, running footsteps. TAPS leaders Jason Hawes and Grant Wilson chased a moving shadow into a room that had no other exit—only to find the room empty. "We've had experiences before where we've come face to face with stuff, but not in that way," Wilson said.

In the torpedo strike area, TAPS technical specialist Steve Gonsalves entreated, "Is there anyone here who lost their life who would like to speak to us? Please give us a sign of your presence." His equipment recorded an instantaneous sharp EMF spike up to 2.2—a remarkably rapid and high reading.

Meanwhile, the North Carolina team's audio equipment picked up a weird, quavering, unidentified voice—garbled as if through some dimensional muffler, but distinguishable nonetheless saying either "ship" or "shipmate," or some related word construct.

After analyzing the data, Jason Hawes reported to the *North Carolina*'s personnel, "You seem to have a spooky and active ship."

Validation is most gratifying, but the investigators certainly were not telling the *North Carolina*'s staff anything they didn't already know.

*   *   *

Both the *North Carolina* and the *Texas* survived not only the smoke and din of war but the wrecking ball as well. They now serve as lasting memories of a cataclysmic century of unprecedented conflict and honor those who bravely rose to the occasion. Within these hallowed hulls, some memories linger in more tangible form, making themselves felt, heard, seen, or all of the above—memories that cannot quite let go of this physical plane. And the *Texas* and the *North Carolina* are not the only battleships of the dead; one such vessel is the vanguard of all the rest, at the epicenter of one of the U.S. Navy's saddest hours.

Echoes of Infamy

The foul weather was their friend. Oppressive clouds and churning seas helped cloak their advance across the Pacific far from the shipping lanes and under radio silence. Their audacious undertaking required surprise, and they managed to maintain that across four thousand miles of ocean and twelve tense days. Six aircraft carriers, two battleships, three cruisers, and nine destroyers—the strike force was the cream of the Imperial Japanese Navy. On December 6, 1941, the eve of the attack, a relic sacred to all Japanese sailors was brought forth: the ensign from the flagship at the 1904 Battle of Tsushima Strait, the glorious victory that had announced to the world that Japan's sea force had come of age. The Tsushima battle ensign was hoisted anew in hope that it would wave over another great triumph on the morrow.

And so on December 7 the early Sunday morning calm of Pearl Harbor, Hawaii, was shattered by the roar of nearly two hundred Japanese aircraft—torpedo bombers, dive bombers, fighter planes—bringing hell on the wing to the headquarters of the U.S. Pacific Fleet. Within minutes the placid moorings of Battleship Row between Ford Island and the harbor shore erupted in deafening explosions followed by fire, shouts, and billowing blackness. An armor-piercing bomb plowed into the forward magazine of the USS *Arizona* and ripped her apart with seismic force, setting off fires that burned for days and raining black, acrid debris down on Ford Island and the harbor. The *Arizona*, a *Pennsylvania*-class battleship of 1915 vintage, had come out to Pearl Harbor in 1940 as part of the fleet sent to be a forward deterrent to Japanese aggression. Now the *Arizona* became the first victim of that aggression on the "day of infamy" that brought the United States into World War II. Her captain, Franklin Van Valkenburgh, died with her, as did Rear Adm. Isaac C. Kidd, commander of Battleship Division I; he was the first flag officer to die in the Pacific war. Both would receive posthumous Medals of Honor. Seven more bombs struck the *Arizona* as she sank, and destruction rained down on the six battleships arrayed alongside her. Down went the *California*, slammed by two bomb hits. Three torpedoes smashed into the *Oklahoma* and capsized her. The *West Virginia* sank, as did the *Nevada*, the only one of the ships to get under way before being hit. The *Maryland* and *Tennessee* suffered damage as well. The Japanese attacked in two waves, taking out airfields and buildings as well as the unfortunate seven vessels on Battleship Row. Hickam Airfield, headquarters of the Pacific Air Forces, was hit hard; soldiers died at their breakfast. More than half of the Army, Navy, and Marine aircraft sitting on Hickam and Ford Island airfields were destroyed.

As the inferno raged all around, the senior surviving officer on the *Arizona* rallied his remaining crew and sought to contain the flames tearing through his sinking ship. Lt. Cdr. Samuel G. Fuqua later received the Medal of Honor for his lifesaving actions on that blackest of days. A sergeant of the *Arizona's* Marine detachment later said that Fuqua's "calmness gave me courage, and I looked around to see if I could help." Fuqua managed to get the survivors clear by just after 10:30 AM, and the *Arizona* was abandoned, still flaming, still smoking, settling into the berth that she occupies to this day.

The battle ensign of Tsushima had brought good fortune to the Japanese, who lost fewer than thirty planes while bringing cataclysmic destruction to the foe. Most of the 2,403 American servicemen who were killed that morning were Navy personnel, and the 1,177 men (out of a crew of 1,512) who perished on the *Arizona* formed the majority of the Navy's losses.

Japan's tactically brilliant but strategically ill-conceived gambit brought the unfettered wrath of America roaring into the war. The carnage of Pearl Harbor left a lasting mark on the national psyche, and the location of the tragedy continues to reverberate with the metaphysical aftershocks that untimely deaths bestow. It is little wonder that Pearl Harbor has been ranked as one of America's "Top Ten Most Haunted Battlefields." From Ford Island to the *Arizona's* resting place to Hickam Field, and in the maze of military buildings in between, reports have surfaced for years of rampant and varied paranormal activity. Voices speak in empty rooms. Footsteps sound where no living foot now treads. A glowing mass of humanoid phosphorescence drifts among the residential quarters of the naval complex. The sad, lost ghost of a young boy wanders in an eternal quest for his parents. Shadowy wraiths of uniformed men tread on Ford Island. Worst of all is the muted, faded noise of explosions, of bombs falling, auditory scars that never healed, the echoes of infamy.

Hickam Air Force Base, where so many perished so suddenly that morning, has been haunted ever since. Hallways ring to the sound of invisible stomping feet in concert with invisible keychain jingle-jangle. A bathroom faucet turns itself on. Big, sturdy glass doors open inexplicably and proceed to flail closed and open and closed and open again with mad rage.

But the mostly submerged hulk of the battleship *Arizona* is the epicenter of Pearl Harbor's haunted quadrant. The flag still flies above her, and all passing Navy ships salute it. Since 1962, when the memorial span was built to straddle her sorrowful mass, thousands have made the pilgrimage to pay tribute. Hundreds of sailors are entombed in the sunken leviathan, which to this day still bleeds oil from her old wounds. To any visitor it is a place of profound, powerful solemnity. To those sensitive to the presence of spirits it is a cacophonous nexus of voices, explosions, and resident souls who are both observable and communicative.

One psychic who visited on a sunny day of picture-book tropical beauty recalled, "I seemed to be the only one aware of the many hundreds of spirits calling out to anyone who could see them. The heavy sadness there broke my heart and seemed so at opposites with the peaceful day." Her first inklings came near the memorial entrance, where she saw "pixilated lights dancing near a palm tree. I knew that a spirit was coming forward." Soon, as if other spirits were keying in on her attuned presence, "more distortions began to appear all around me and I began hearing desperate whisperings." They clamored around her, so "eager to get news to their loved ones" that she experienced extrasensory overload. She came to the conclusion that the individuals in the vociferous ghost crew either had "the need to finish some important business" or had in some cases simply "left behind a residual energy imprinted on the area at the time of their passing."

If such is the forcefulness of the haunted vibrations above the wreck, one can imagine how powerfully the aura must radiate below the surface, down in the mangled topography of the grave ship. It is simultaneously an overpowering and ethereal sensation, one well known to Dan Lenihan, who from 1983 to 2001 made multiple dives around the wreck for the National Park Service's Submerged Resource Center. The first field seasons of the *Arizona* Preservation Project in the 1980s focused on examining the wreckage and producing line drawings. The 608-foot battleship was at the time the largest underwater object ever mapped. "For the diver, *Arizona* emerges from the gloom as some surreal metallic structure of monstrous proportions," Lenihan later wrote. He noted that the members of his underwater team, Navy divers and Park Service divers alike, all went from being "at first overwhelmed with the ship" to eventually becoming "obsessed by it." The wreck can enthrall even the most dispassionate scientific mind. Here lie the giant remains of a giant tragedy. It is more than just a mass of steel to be measured, quantified, and analyzed. It is a crypt, twisted and torn, exuding despair, inspiring reverential awe. "There's something," observed Lenihan, "about experiencing the scene of a violent act while swimming underwater."

The ship has exerted her haunting power virtually since smoke still rose from her battered form. The first reports of hauntings at the *Arizona* wreck site began during World War II. Sailors passing the wreckage in the harbor spoke in hushed tones of how the ship had been cursed from the beginning because she was christened with a bottle of water instead of wine (the tradition-violating gesture a nod to puritanical Navy Secretary Josephus Daniels' banning of all drinking in the Navy). There were sightings of a ghost patrolling on the exposed deck at low tide, a ghost on lookout at the flagpole, a nocturnally active ghost still visible in the predawn grayness. Sailors' lore quickly ascribed all these appearances to one particular spirit, that of a guilt-ridden officer of the deck who, on the morning of the attack, had abandoned his station momentarily to attend to some triviality and died in the initial explosion that sank his ship. But is it reasonable to believe that all of the many spectral appearances belong to a single entity at a spot so heavily laden with the burden of massive violent death, a spot where more than a thousand young men were killed in one grim morning? One only has to recall the multitude of desperate souls who inundated the psychic who ventured into their sphere. It is also worth noting that, regardless of the time of day or angle of perspective, the *Arizona* can have a strange effect on photography, and that camera-wielding tourists at the memorial frequently find eerie orbs and shadowy shapes hovering in their snapshots.

"There are ghosts on the *Arizona*, whose presence you feel when you are alone, particularly in the hours at dusk," Lenihan wrote. "But they don't frighten me. I feel a strange kinship with them; they make me sad—sad that they never got to be heroes, or fools, or anything else." Reminded of the film *Unforgiven*, in which Clint Eastwood's character ruminates about the taking of human life, Lenihan offered a paraphrase for the *Arizona*'s dead: "That bomb took away not only what they were but everything they were ever going to be."

In one day at Pearl Harbor, Japan succeeded in destroying the battleships of the U.S. Pacific Fleet. Tsushima's battle ensign indeed waved once again on a day of Japanese victory. But it was a hollow victory. Most of the American battleships would be salvaged, repaired, and put back into the fight. Furthermore, the ships that would prove most crucial in the coming Pacific struggle were away from Pearl Harbor that fateful day. Japan would come to regret not waiting to strike until the U.S. Navy's aircraft carriers had returned to the target zone.

* * *

In the emerging conflict, the aircraft carrier would prove to be the most valuable chess piece in naval warfare. The flood tide of Japanese conquest was halted at last in the Battle of the Coral Sea (May 7–8, 1942), history's first carrier-versus-carrier duel, and the first sea battle ever fought in which the combatant warships never saw each other. The turning point in the Pacific followed at the Battle of Midway (June 3–7, 1942), another clash of carriers that produced one of the U.S. Navy's greatest and most decisive victories. The fate of the war was dictated in a titanic showdown over a tiny atoll a thousand miles west of Hawaii. Japan desired Midway as a perimeter extension; the United States sought to hold it at all costs and roll back the Japanese advance. Japan lost not only the battle but four carriers and a host of its finest pilots as well. After Midway, Japan would never again know the dominance it had held in the opening months of the Pacific war.

Midway Atoll is no longer under the aegis of the U.S. Navy; it is administered by the U.S. Fish and Wildlife Service. Where thousands of Navy and Marine personnel once dwelled there remains a ghost town of abandoned, decaying buildings and empty streets. A handful of residents—contract workers and their families, mainly, plus wildlife refuge staff—share the remote outcropping with thousands of seabirds. As the locus of one of the most important naval engagements in history, Midway is, fittingly, a national historic landmark, though an isolated and rarely visited one, a speck in the vast Pacific expanse. But those who do live or pass through here offer consistent descriptions of a frequently seen ghost, a cigarette-smoking specter in military uniform.

Described as "a quiet, contemplative man," he has been spotted outside the former bachelor officers' quarters, near the old theater, and around the old water tower. A contract employee who spied him in front of the old BOQ showed up at work "mad because the military guy didn't return his greeting." But no "military guy" was stationed on Midway anymore. Another contract employee and his wife living in a house near the old barracks had to move because she became so upset by the specter's presence, especially after talking to others who had seen him. Their new quarters were as far away from the ghost's haunting grounds as it was possible to get. A couple of American jetliner pilots who were transporting an empty plane to Thailand also encountered the spectral smoker when they stopped at Midway to refuel. One of them remarked to the manager of the wildlife refuge, "I didn't know you still had military here." They too were upset because the man had not returned their greeting.

It was nothing personal. He is simply a stoic ghost, prone to meditative tobacco smoke and long gazes seaward, where mighty aircraft carriers once cut across the waves and their bombers filled the sky, determining the course of history.

Where the Midway ghost fixes his eternal stare, the carriers rose to their epochal moment. They would grow in number to meet the Pacific challenge. And some would become part of naval history's haunted fleet.

Blue-Eyed Charlie and Shadow Ed

Tokyo Rose, the silken-voiced World War II radio propagandist for
Japan, is credited with coining a ship's nickname that has with-
stood the test of time. When she dubbed the USS *Lexington* "the
Blue Ghost," the name was doubly appropriate. First, the aircraft carrier's
dark blue camouflage paint enabled the gigantic vessel to appear seemingly
out of nowhere; second, the Japanese showed a marked tendency, born no
doubt of wishful thinking, to offer premature reports of the feared ship's
demise. Four times they declared the *Lexington* sunk, and four times they
were wrong; the carrier that wreaked such havoc on the Japanese navy survived the Pacific conflict and several decades of postwar service to become
in her retirement years a treasured piece of floating history. Since 1992
crowds have streamed to the waterfront at Corpus Christi, Texas, to visit
one of the Navy's most celebrated aircraft carriers, to traverse the massive
flight deck, to wend through the labyrinth of passageways, to touch the
remnants of an adventurous past.

But some of the remnants are of a more ethereal nature—visible but
not tangible, talkative but elusive, there and suddenly not there. In her half-
century of service the *Lexington* housed many crews and absorbed hundreds
of deaths, and spirits are astir in her cavernous reaches. In response to the
alarming prevalence of ghostly sightings, the *Corpus Christi Caller-Times*
set up a Web site where distraught witnesses could exorcise the memories of their experiences. The site soon swelled with some two hundred
reports by visitors to the *Lexington* who had come face to face with the
paranormal. On this sixteen-deck floating city, ghosts have been encountered above, below, and in between, vestiges of different time periods and
disparate tragedies. One particular apparition, however, has made himself
especially familiar to the living who venture on his ship. Descriptions of
him are consistent in details of both temperament and deportment. He has

been characterized as singularly "polite, knowledgeable and kind." And he is handsome as the devil, cutting quite a dash in his Navy summer whites, fair-haired and youthful. But above all there are the eyes—unforgettably, piercingly blue. Interestingly, the Blue Ghost has a blue-eyed ghost.

Who is this charming, affable specter? The candidates are legion. The *Lexington* logged her first death before ever entering the theater of war, a poignant death that shocked the nation. Many more quickly followed in the Pacific cauldron, and yet more entered the roll call of the fallen during the ship's ensuing years of service. Some stay, occasionally crossing into our realm from theirs; foremost among them is the friendly, mysterious, good-looking hologram with the azure stare. Though who he was in life remains cloaked in uncertainty's mist, his familiar presence has earned him a nickname; lacking more concrete data, those who have seen him simply call him "Charlie."

The ship he haunts is the fifth in the Navy's history to be dubbed *Lexington* in honor of the village where American Minutemen first met British Redcoats in battle on April 19, 1775. More specifically, this *Lexington* carried the torch of her immediate predecessor, the aircraft carrier lost in the Battle of the Coral Sea. The *Lexington* that was launched in February 1943 was of the superlative new *Essex* class, one of two dozen such carriers that surged forth from American shipyards to help win the war. She was 880 feet long at the waterline, 910 feet at the flight deck—a flight deck large enough for three simultaneous football games. More than two acres of takeoff and landing surface sat atop 27,100 tons of U.S. diplomacy, the exemplar of a new era of warships. As tall as a nineteen-story building and as long as three city blocks, she set a course for her Caribbean shakedown cruise amid a general spirit of élan from bridge to belowdecks. On her sailed a young recruit beloved by the American public, a celebrity who was imbued with that rarest of celebrity commodities: a heart of gold and a lack of guile.

Lt. Nile Clark Kinnick Jr. was more than just a promising flyer. He was "the Cornbelt Comet" himself, the All-America halfback who captained the University of Iowa Hawkeyes through their legendary 1939 season— Kinnick the Ironman, the Big Ten's Most Valuable Player, the Heisman Trophy winner, the Associated Press' Top Male Athlete of 1939. He epitomized the scholar-warrior ideal, a book-devouring Phi Beta Kappa and student body president as well as football hero. His teammates loved him. The press and the public loved him. His Heisman Trophy acceptance

speech at the Downtown Athletic Club in New York City was so moving
that the audience momentarily sat in stunned silence before rising from
their seats in an eruption of thunderous applause, whistles, and cheers. A
reporter observed, "You realized the ovation wasn't alone for Nile Kinnick,
the outstanding college football player of the year. It was also for Nile
Kinnick, typifying everything admirable in American youth. This country's
OK as long as it produces Nile Kinnicks. The football part is incidental."

Kinnick brought Iowa its only Heisman. His jersey number, 24, was
retired, and Kinnick Stadium today is the proud home of Hawkeye football tradition. His statue, with books in his hand and a football helmet at
his feet, greets all who enter.

He was interested in an eventual career in politics, but law school had
to be put aside for flight school; he had already enlisted in the Naval Air
Corps Reserve before the bombs fell on Pearl Harbor. Embarking for war,
Kinnick wrote in his diary, "May God give me the courage and ability to
so conduct myself in every situation that my country, my family and my
friends will be proud of me."

Even amid the rigors of flight training he was aware of the beauty
that was all around for those who looked for it. "I flew up in the clouds
today—tall, voluminous cumulus clouds," he told his diary. "They were like
snow-covered mountains, range after range of them. I felt like an alpine
adventurer, climbing up their canyons, winding my way between their
peaks—a billowy fastness, a celestial citadel."

Nile Kinnick was killed on June 2, 1943, when his Grumman F4F
Wildcat bled oil during airborne training exercises off the coast of
Venezuela. He was still four miles from the *Lexington* when the leak
became a draining gush. He knew that even if he could make it back, the
ship's flight deck was crowded with other planes waiting to take off. Trying
to land there would imperil them all. He executed an emergency drop-
down in the water. When the rescue party arrived at his downed plane less
than ten minutes later, Kinnick was gone. He had been twenty-four years
old. His body was never found.

In old photographs he is still brimming with life. A warm smile lights
his wholesome chiseled features, his pale eyes are intense with the enthusiasm and moxie of youth, eyes afire with a young man's dreams—dreams
never to be realized. His death stunned the country and served as a grim
reminder that military service, even when not being carried out before the
enemy's guns, is extremely dangerous; and that life, even the life of a soar-

ing exemplar, is as tenuous and fragile as an eggshell. "I never had a shock like that in my life," one of Kinnick's teammates later reminisced. "Hell, I thought he was going to live forever."

"There was just an aura about him," another friend recalled. "He didn't try to create it, it was just there. You really had the feeling you were in the presence of someone special."

In the service, the adage wisely observes, all give some, and some give all. Kinnick's loss hovered like a mournful harbinger on the *Lexington*, but before much time had passed, the sad memory would become subsumed into the mounting death toll of a ship in wartime. In the thick of heavy night action off Kwajalein, a torpedo plowed into the *Lexington*'s starboard side on December 4, 1943, killing 9 crewmen and wounding 35. Off Luzon, a kamikaze pilot emphatically fulfilled his one-way mission on November 5, 1944, crashing into the *Lexington*'s island structure in a flowering blaze of destruction and death. Fifty sailors were killed and 130 were wounded in the suicide plane's fiery hit. Embroiled in the Pacific's biggest sea battles for twenty-one months, the *Lexington* ultimately suffered 238 deaths (a total that would near the 300 mark by the conclusion of her duties).

But in the end, the *Lexington* gave worse than she got. From the Battle of the Philippine Sea and the "Great Marianas Turkey Shoot" to the climactic Battle of Leyte Gulf, from the China Sea to Tokyo Bay (where she was the first U.S. carrier to enter), the *Lexington* earned her stature as enemy's bane. Her planes helped eliminate Japan's naval air arm and were in on the sinking of many of the mightiest of the Japanese battleships, cruisers, and carriers. She sank or destroyed 300,000 tons of enemy cargo and damaged an additional 600,000 tons. Her guns shot down 15 enemy aircraft and assisted in splashing 5 more, while her deadeye pilots eradicated 372 Japanese planes in flight and another 475 on the ground. And, belying the hopeful pronouncements of Tokyo Rose, the Blue Ghost survived it all.

After eight years of reserve-fleet status, during which time she was refitted with an angled flight deck and other requisite upgrades, the *Lexington* was recommissioned in 1955. The first carrier to deploy air-to-surface missiles, she was standing by for whatever might ensue during the tense moments of the 1959 Laotian Crisis and the 1962 Cuban Missile Crisis. In the 1960s she emerged as an important training ship for Navy and Marine aviators vital to the Vietnam War effort, and in 1967 the

Lexington logged her 200,000th arrested landing. Her service outlasted the Vietnam years, and in 1980 she became the first ship in the history of the U.S. Navy to have women stationed aboard as crew members. When she was finally decommissioned in 1991, the venerable *Lexington* had the twin distinctions of being the last active survivor of the *Essex* class and America's longest-serving aircraft carrier.

A long time can equal a lot of ghosts; even if less than one-tenth of the *Lexington*'s three hundred dead still linger, that amounts to a significantly haunted ship. The spectral sightings predate the ship's museum years by a wide margin. A sailor who served on the *Lexington* in 1969–70 reported friendly interactions with a ghost in the aft engine room (where men perished in the 1943 torpedo strike), and the "Charlie" nickname for the prominent resident spirit was an established part of the ship's lore by at least the early 1980s. Sailors described the entity as "friendly and harmless," though no doubt rather unsettling on first encounter.

Run-ins with Charlie and other denizens of the shadow realm increased concomitantly with the increase in foot traffic after the *Lexington* was opened to the public. A couple visiting from Peoria, Illinois, were pleased to be greeted by a nice young man in uniform who offered to give them a tour of the ship. He led them below, all the while affable and informative, particularly about the workings of the engine room. But he disappeared before the couple had a chance to thank him. On leaving the ship, they made a point of tracking down another staffer to express their appreciation for "that knowledgeable young sailor" who had shown them around. The staffer, David Deal, himself a *Lexington* veteran, stood there aghast. He looked as if he had seen a ghost because he had just been told about one. He charged below, searching the engine room and environs in vain for the nonexistent tour guide. The confused couple described the mystery man in more detail: fair-haired, a pleasing smile, quite handsome. The most remarkable blue eyes.

"This apparition told things about the engine that I didn't even know," said Deal.

But Charlie isn't always so loquacious. A woman in a tour group being led through the engine room fell back from the crowd to read some exhibit signage. She began to feel distinctly uneasy, as if being watched. She turned and he was standing right behind her: a sailor in a smart white dress uniform, young-looking, fair, his hypnotic eyes focused on her like twin blue laser beams. She started with a jolt, and he was gone. The woman grabbed her son from amid the tourist throng and asked if he too had seen the strange sailor. No, he hadn't. The museum volunteer leading the tour confessed that she had not seen the figure either. Nor had anyone else. Except the mystified woman—and who knows how many others over the years.

Who is Charlie? The rhetorical "who" is the salient curiosity with any haunting, but all the more so with a spirit so vivid and interactive as the *Lexington* charmer. His attractive appearance and winning personality are remarkably suggestive of Nile Kinnick, the ship's first—not to mention most famous—fatality. But Kinnick was a flyer, and Charlie's interests and expertise are more indicative of an engine room stalwart, lending credence to the school of thought that he is the ectoplasmic vestige of one of those killed in the Kwajalein torpedo tragedy. Whoever he is, he is not alone. In addition to fair-haired, blue-eyed, crisply attired Charlie there is a dark-haired ghost in jeans and a denim work shirt who has been spotted making a precipitous jump from one deck down to the next, only to vanish in thin air. Members of the museum staff have seen a Japanese pilot and an American sailor appear simultaneously and then, when approached, disappear in the same fashion—twin hauntings, most likely, from the 1944 kamikaze inferno. One poor tourist recounted to a staff member how a khaki-clad officer appeared before him near the galley and barked at him to take off his baseball cap, then promptly disappeared.

And if Charlie is in fact the spirit of a sailor laid low by a Japanese torpedo, he is not the only lingering remnant of that midnight catastrophe. There is another presence in the engine room markedly different from the welcoming Charlie; this one is unseen and manifests itself with seething hostility, slamming doors, killing lights, seemingly desirous of repelling visitors rather than accommodating them as Charlie does. When this negative energy is afoot, a sudden temperature drop chills the air and there is the noise of frantic movement in the engine room blackness.

Everyone from sailors to high-ranking museum staff to visitors has experienced the unmistakable little sounds of human proximity—the rustle of clothes, the increasingly loud cadence of approaching footsteps—only to pivot and realize that no one is there. The sensation of someone rushing past, the clip-clop of hard-soled shoes hurrying along deserted passageways, lights turning on and off with unnerving poltergeist abandon, heavy sliding metal doors opening and closing repeatedly and violently, covers being pulled off the beds of overnight visitors consigned to the cold sweat of insomnia until morning's blessed arrival.

Navy cadets on a *Lexington* overnighter emboldened one another into a nocturnal dare; they rose from their berths and proceeded to run around the dark, empty ship. And they ran headlong into a ghost. The face of a long-dead sailor blocked their path, forcing a retreat on the double-quick.

A pair of staffers was making the rounds when a man's voice shouted, "Hey!" The incident was unusual only in that there was no one else on board the ship at the moment. A museum volunteer stared with a mixture of wonderment and bewilderment as a sailor walked right through a bulkhead. A door had once been there, and the ghost was retracing his well-worn steps impervious to the altered landscape. Similarly defying the laws of physics, a man in a World War II–era uniform has appeared and then slowly dissolved back into invisibility.

The carrier's ghosts run the gamut from vivid and detailed to undulating and blurry. A ship's electrician in the primary flight control tower saw a weird glowing blue ball that hovered above the flight deck and then suddenly shot into the dark sky. A blinding flash of red similarly appeared in another staff member's office.

Regardless of the relative clarity of the manifestations, most seem to offer tantalizing clues linking them to specific catastrophic events. A damage control officer on duty one night as a storm raged watched in disbelief as lightning illuminated the night sky to reveal the ghosts of long-dead men scurrying across the flight deck amid a cacophony of desperate screams.

Screams are a recurrent motif of *Lexington* paranormal reports—screams, voices (sometimes one, sometimes two in a heated argument), dim sounds of firing weaponry.

Some areas of the ship—the switch room, for example—are redolent with a pall of despair that is unbearable to the psychically sensitive. Reactions have ranged from fearful agitation to a panicked need to leave immediately to outright physical illness.

Sometimes, it is not so much a question of terror as just downright mystification. A restoration work crew in the midst of a paint job returned from a coffee break to find the work completed. In another coffee-break phenomenon, a worker mopped the fo'c'sle, went to the hangar deck for some java, and came back to find a fresh set of footprints in the middle of the still-wet deck—but with no footprints coming in or going out, a macabre and logic-defying head-scratcher worthy of a Charles Addams cartoon.

* * *

In another port, in another state, another aircraft carrier lives out her retirement years as a popular destination for history-loving travelers. The *Lexington* and her sister ship, the USS *Yorktown*, have much in common. Both are *Essex*-class carriers. Just as the *Lexington* was named to honor her predecessor, sunk in the Battle of the Coral Sea, the *Yorktown* was so dubbed to keep afloat the legacy of the carrier *Yorktown* lost at the Battle of Midway. The new *Lexington* and the new *Yorktown* fought (at times alongside one another) in World War II, went through a brief decommissioning hiatus, were recommissioned and refitted in the 1950s, enjoyed noteworthy post–World War II careers, and ended up as floating museums. And both are haunted. But there the similarities end. For while the salient ghost among the *Lexington*'s ethereal crew is the friendly, accommodating Charlie, the principal spirit encamped on the *Yorktown* is a skulking, secretive, and sometimes malevolent wraith. Officers of the security department at Patriot's Point in Charleston, South Carolina (home of the *Yorktown* and other historic Navy vessels), long ago bestowed the ghost with a nickname befitting his personality: "Shadow Ed."

Like Charlie on the *Lexington*, Shadow Ed is not the *Yorktown*'s sole spectral occupant. Nor should it be at all surprising that, as in the case of the *Lexington*, a warship with the *Yorktown*'s valorous record picked up a ghost or two along the way. They didn't call her "the Fighting Lady" for nothing. Launched and commissioned in early 1943, the *Yorktown* was in the thick of things before the year ended, platforming raids in support of the assault on the Gilbert Islands in November. Early 1944 found her in Task Group 58 alongside the *Lexington* and others carrying out Operation Flintlock—mission: the Marshall Islands. Throughout the spring she cut an ever-widening swath through the seas of war, south to New Guinea to support Gen. Douglas MacArthur's Hollandia assault, north to the Marianas to back the Saipan and Guam landings—and to lend her might to the Battle of the Philippine Sea. In the battle's first day alone the planes of the Fighting Lady splashed thirty-seven enemy aircraft and dumped twenty-one tons of bombs on the airfields of Guam.

By January 1945 the carrier was tightening the noose on Japan and fighting her way up the South China Sea, where her planes sank an astounding forty-four enemy ships. By March she was striking air bases on Japan's home islands and incurring heavy punishment as a result. Shooting down attacking Japanese planes port and starboard, the *Yorktown*'s gunners finally let one slip through on March 18. The Japanese bomber's payload hit the signal bridge and ripped through the deck before exploding, blowing two large holes in the hull, killing five men and wounding twenty-six. Through it all, the carrier's antiaircraft guns kept blasting away, finally nailing the bomber that had scored the hit. The *Yorktown* was wounded but still operational. The Japanese had failed to sink her, and within a month she herself would be in on a sinking of epic and historic proportions.

The *Yamato*, the greatest battleship ever built, the symbol of Japanese sea power, lumbered forth at the head of a task force in early April 1945 in a quixotic last-ditch ploy to stem the tide at Okinawa. For the giant ship as for her homeland, it was an all-or-nothing gesture; the *Yamato* advanced with only enough fuel for a one-way trip. It was all she would need. The *Yorktown* joined in on the attack on April 7; naval aviation sank the *Yamato*, and with her died the battleship era and the hopes of Japan.

Forged in the fires of World War II, the *Yorktown* would come to be associated with another war as well. In retrospect, the Fighting Lady's prominent presence in the Vietnam conflict can be seen as the culmination of a continuum of Far East involvement. She was there for a show of force in the Taiwan Strait when the Chinese Communists bombed the Nationalist-held islands of Quemoy and Matsu in 1958–59. She deployed repeatedly to Vietnamese waters as the communist guerrilla insurgency ratcheted the instability level in 1959–60. She took part in Operation Sea Serpent, antisubmarine warfare exercises conducted by the Southeast Asian Treaty Organization, in 1962–63. And in 1964–65, while Vietnam still remained a tangential issue to mainstream America, the *Yorktown* was back in the South China Sea, her old World War II hunting grounds, conducting special operations as U.S. involvement in the Vietnamese civil war rapidly escalated. And from 1966 to 1968, as the United States entered the fray full-bore and Vietnam's faraway internecine nightmare became the Vietnam War of newspaper front pages and evening-news TV screens, the *Yorktown* did six Vietnamese tours of duty with Task Force 77. By the time the American public fully awakened to the situation, the *Yorktown* had been confronting it for years.

A couple of relatively glamorous assignments—recovery ship for the *Apollo 8* space mission and a stand-in role in the movie dramatization of Pearl Harbor, *Tora! Tora! Tora!*—came the *Yorktown*'s way before her 1970 decommissioning and 1975 dedication as a museum ship. At miscellaneous points during her long, varied, and laudatory career the ghosts that now haunt her took up residence. In surveying the *Yorktown* hauntings, one cannot help but notice the intriguing symmetry between her dynamic, multilayered service record and the eclectic, multifaceted body of her ghost lore.

Occult experiences have ranged from familial telepathy across generations to phenomenal photographic evidence, from auditory anomalies and inexplicable sightings of phantom figures to the smothering cloak of raw terror that a ghost's mere presence can cast upon the poor soul burdened with sensitivity to supernatural power spots. First and foremost on the paranormalist's line of inquiry must be the enigmatic Shadow Ed: from what period of the ship's history does he hail?

The evidence is tantalizingly scant; a Patriot's Point security officer described Shadow Ed as "a dark shadow-like figure that stands about five foot six inches." Multiple staffers have spied him lurking around the second deck, near the officers' quarters on the starboard side. He darts in the passageway but is gone if pursued. Those who have worked the graveyard shift on the big, empty ship know well the cold chill that accompanies an unexpected glimpse of Shadow Ed.

A tourist observed a ghost matching that (admittedly shadowy) description near the engine room. The "dark outline of a person" emerged, appeared to pick up an object, stared at something momentarily, then merged back into obscurity. The witness' first thought was that a homeless person had stowed away, but she quickly realized that the figure, though humanoid in form, had no discernible details of clothing, coloration, hair—he was, in short, a "shadow person," and as he blended back into the larger shadows, the witness found herself wondering, "Why didn't he make any noise?" The engine room yielded another compelling clue in the *Yorktown* ghost mystery when a photographer with a digital camera snapped a picture that shows the vague, translucent form of a man in what appears to be a khaki uniform.

Other manifestations may or may not represent the same specter: footsteps, voices, pans clattering in the unoccupied galley—are these more hints of the shadow person or the percussive resonances of disparate residual spirits? And what of the pall of horror that besets certain visitors? A woman spending the weekend on the *Yorktown* as part of a group trip had just showered and was standing before the mirror when she felt a jolt of raw, animal fear—immediate, instinctive, and unmistakable. Someone . . . something was standing behind her. Too petrified to raise her eyes to the mirror, she didn't bother to gather her things as she fled. A heavy metal door groaned open as she ran past it. The presence, she said, was overpowering and best described as "ominous."

Less baleful yet all the more mystifying was the experience of a vacationer who visited the *Yorktown* on a whim, only to be bowled over once on board by "the feeling that something or someone was attempting to contact me." On the hangar deck he discovered a memorial list, and on it was the name of a cousin of whom he had heard but had never met. His cousin and the young man's comrades (also on the memorial) had never made it back from a Guam sortie in 1944. No one in the visitor's family had ever mentioned what ship he had served on, and the vacationer himself had no prior knowledge of the connection. That this long-lost cousin who died while serving on the *Yorktown* had the first name "Edward" is entirely coincidental—or is it?

The *Yorktown* certainly earned her ghosts, but Navy stories claim that at least some of the spirits were inherited from the previous *Yorktown*. According to the yarn, a couple of sailors were playing cards in the engine room of the older *Yorktown* when she was sunk at the Battle of Midway. Once the new *Yorktown* launched, these card-playing dead from the earlier ship moved in, made themselves at home, and continue to play cards, stuck forever in the game they were playing when they were sent to a watery grave.

* * *

Can spirits from one ship latch on to another out of some spectral logic of affinity? Can a new ship's name invite restless spirits rendered homeless by their old ship's destruction? If a ship's name can in fact serve as a spirit magnet, it could help explain one of the most unusual cases in the haunted history of the U.S. Navy, a case involving fraternal bonds that held fast from America's heartland to beyond the realm of the living.

Brothers to the End, and Beyond

The white frame house at 98 Adams Street in Waterloo, Iowa, was conveniently located next to a vacant lot. Mrs. Sullivan, hoping to keep her walls and floors intact, was glad to have a place where she could shoo her five boys outside to play. They were a high-spirited posse who liked to stick together, and that vacant lot was like the Sullivan Brothers Sports Arena while they were growing up.

Now that the two oldest, George and Frank, were back from their hitches in the Navy, the gang was all together again, working down at the meat-packing plant and helping the family make ends meet. Their father, Thomas F. Sullivan, was a freight conductor for the Illinois Central Railroad. Their mother, Alleta Abel Sullivan, had tied the knot with Tom at St. Joseph's Catholic Church in 1914, and the couple had wasted no time in starting a family, a big family. In addition to the boys—George, Frank, Joe, Matt, and Al—there was their sister, Genevieve. And the nuclear family was beginning to sprout offshoots. Al, the youngest, got the jump on his older brothers and was already married and a father; the baby of the family had a baby before the rest of them.

And so life went on in its bustling way in a noisy, cozy house in the middle of Iowa in the middle of America. And then the radio garbled and came in clearly and broadcast a dire report on December 7, 1941, and things would never be the same. The shocking news out of Pearl Harbor became personal for the Sullivans when they found out that Bill Ball—Genevieve's sweetheart and the brothers' good friend—had been killed on the USS *Arizona*. Before a month had passed, the five Sullivans were on their way to Great Lakes Naval Training Center. They had joined the Navy en masse—and on the condition that they not be separated. For the brothers Sullivan, it was all for one and one for all. As one of them put it, "We will make a team together that can't be beat."

They remained dutiful sons all through boot camp and after shipping out, writing frequent letters home to a grateful mother in a suddenly silent house. Their standard sign-off in the correspondence was a cheery, confident, "Keep your chin up." The last mail she received from them was dated November 8, 1942. Then the letters stopped coming.

* * *

At the easternmost extent of the Solomons, Guadalcanal had become a bitterly contested patch of Pacific real estate in late 1942. Anxious to conquer Port Moresby, New Guinea, and thus sever the vital lines of communication and supply between Australia and the American forces, the Japanese began building an air base on Guadalcanal from which to launch raids in support of the Port Moresby push. Not so fast, said the U.S. Marines, who stormed onto Guadalcanal in August, wrested the nascent airstrip from its builders, and converted it to Allied use as Henderson Field. It was a good beginning, but it was only the beginning. Determined Japanese troops remained entrenched on Guadalcanal, and fierce fighting raged into early 1943 as small patches of land were taken, lost, and retaken.

In November 1942 a high-stakes race was on between the Americans and the Japanese as each side attempted to reinforce its own Guadalcanal troops while stopping the foe from doing the same. As American transport ships were unloading on November 12, a Navy task force provided a protective perimeter. Included in this formation was the light cruiser USS *Juneau*. And her ship's roster included five sailors named Sullivan.

The afternoon sky suddenly darkened with thirty Japanese planes that swooped down for the kill. Antiaircraft fire erupted in a deafening staccato rebuttal, shredding the Japanese attack. Only one Japanese plane escaped. The *Juneau* herself shot down a half-dozen torpedo bombers. But the air raid had been only the first wave. After midnight, radar picked up a Japanese naval force—two battleships, a light cruiser, and eleven destroyers—coming in fast past Savo Island. The U.S. Navy steamed forth to meet them with eight destroyers and five cruisers, the *Juneau* among them.

It was an ink black, moonless night, and the vanguard ships in each force were closer to each other than they realized. The order came down to the *Juneau*: "Stand by to open fire." A Japanese searchlight flashed on to reveal the rival formations barely 1,600 yards apart. American destroyer guns roared. Japanese guns answered. American and Japanese ships merged in a brutal, point-blank shootout. Within fifteen minutes the water was aswirl with the detritus of exploding, sinking ships and smoking hulls.

The Naval Battle of Guadalcanal, as it came to be called, was a mere few minutes old when a Japanese torpedo clobbered the port side of the *Juneau* by the forward fire room. The explosion bent the ship, nosing her bow downward and knocking out her power. But the crew managed to keep her limping along, rendezvousing by sunrise with other surviving vessels from the task force. The crippled *Juneau* must have seemed like irresistibly low-hanging fruit to the Japanese submarine that subsequently intercepted her. The submarine's torpedo found its mark on the *Juneau*'s port side near the earlier debilitating wound. And on the morning of Friday the thirteenth, the *Juneau* exploded into two halves; both sank within forty-two seconds, instantly killing the majority of her seven-hundred-man crew.

Frank, Joe, and Matt Sullivan were among the sailors who lost their lives in the torpedo blast.

Al Sullivan, the youngest brother, the one who had a wife and infant son waiting back home, lasted another day before he drowned.

George Sullivan, the first born and the last remaining, kept alive in that hellish sea of sun exposure, thirst, starvation, drowning, and sharks—everywhere sharks—for several more days. Only ten of the approximately one hundred sailors who survived the wreck of the *Juneau* were still alive when the belated rescue teams arrived eight long days later. Those few survivors told of how George Sullivan had kept moving, searching frantically for his brothers from raft to raft, seeking them in vain amid the flotsam and the bodies and the death screams of shark victims. After four or five days, George died too; sharks ate him as he swam off in one final desperate search that he never got to finish.

* * *

"I am writing you in regards to a rumor that my five sons were killed," Alleta Sullivan wrote the Bureau of Naval Personnel in January 1943. "I hated to bother you, but it has worried me so. . . . So please tell me. It was hard to give five sons all at once to the Navy, but I am so proud of my boys that they can serve and help protect their country."

On January 12 the official word arrived. A lieutenant commander, a chief petty officer, and a medical officer intercepted Tom Sullivan at his front door as he was leaving for work.

"I have some news for you about your boys," the commander said.

"Which one?"

"I'm sorry. All five."

A consoling letter from President Franklin D. Roosevelt soon followed, as did a great collective outpouring of public sympathy. Every parent who had a son overseas could only imagine with horror the fivefold grief of the Sullivans. Tom and Alleta had experienced what the Navy determined was "the heaviest loss suffered by a single family in American naval history."

But the Sullivans channeled their bereavement into a gritty determination to soldier on, and by so doing to honor the memory, and the sacrifice, of the five boys. Genevieve Sullivan, the sister, stepped up in a way that surely would have made her brothers proud—she enlisted in the WAVES. Tom and Alleta embarked on a morale-boosting tour of hundreds of shipyards and manufacturing plants, raising money for war bonds and encouraging people on the home front to pitch in on the war effort in whatever way they could. "We can't give up just because the boys are gone," Alleta said. "We've got to keep things moving here at home." Smiling through her tears, the mother recalled, "The boys always wrote at the end of their letters, 'Keep your chin up.' And now's a good time to do just that."

At St. Patrick's Cathedral in New York City, where a solemn mass was held in honor of the Sullivan brothers, Father Joseph Flannelly greeted Tom and Alleta at the door. "I have received kings and queen and premiers," he said, "but no one has been more welcome here than Mrs. Sullivan." After the services, Archbishop Francis J. Spellman presented the Sullivans with rosary beads and a silver medal that Pope Pius XII himself had sent from the Vatican. Said the archbishop, "I know of no one else who deserves them more."

On April 4, 1943, Alleta Sullivan stood on the San Francisco waterfront to christen a new *Fletcher*-class destroyer—the USS *The Sullivans*. It was the first Navy ship to be named after more than one person, the first to have "*The*" as part of the name. The ship's official motto was the selfsame motto of the five Sullivan brothers: "We stick together."

The Sullivans screened the mighty carriers in the air assaults on Kwajalein in January 1944, then fought onward across the central Pacific as Allied forces pushed the Japanese back through the Caroline Islands, the Palaus, the Marianas, and Okinawa to the Japanese mainland. The shamrock of Ireland was emblazoned proudly on the destroyer's forward stack. Miraculously, through all the action she encountered in World War

II and beyond, *The Sullivans* never suffered a single death on board. Good luck ran with her; it was as if a protecting Celtic spirit, or spirits, watched over her.

The Korean War offers a compelling example. It was Christmas Day 1952. The guns of *The Sullivans* were scoring bull's-eyes in their efforts to blow up a railroad bridge, arousing the wrath of the enemy artillery on shore, which opened up with a vengeance. An astounding fifty rounds from the Communists' guns utterly failed to scratch the lucky destroyer; near-misses rained down all around her, but not one scored a hit. *The Sullivans'* gunners answered in kind, delivering destruction to the shore artillery.

The ship lent her shamrock presence to various volatile Cold War scenarios—the Marine landings at Beirut in 1958, the naval blockade during the Cuban Missile Crisis in 1962—before being decommissioned in 1965. In 1977 she was donated to the city of Buffalo, New York, where she remains on view as part of the Buffalo and Erie County Naval and Servicemen's Park. The spirit, or spirits, that protected *The Sullivans* when she sailed in harm's way remain with her now in her retirement; and they are not averse to making their presence known.

While the paranormal activity on *The Sullivans* seems particularly acute on Friday the thirteenth, the date the *Juneau* went down with all five Sullivan brothers on board, ghostly manifestations have by no means been limited to that unsettling spot on the calendar. One former volunteer, an avowed skeptic regarding the supernatural, admitted to having had "weird experiences" on the ship that "freaked him out": conversations overheard when no one else was on board, the sounds of footsteps when the ship was empty, the nerve-jangling noise of chains being dragged. Mystified night watchmen speak of lights turning on and off by themselves as well as other electricity-related oddities, of locked doors being unlocked (while the watchman has the only key), of objects being thrown about, of hatches opening. Disparate weird yet distinctly identifiable auditory hauntings have been reported: the sporting ghosts engage in nocturnal craps games and card games on *The Sullivans*. Disturbingly, a voice out of nowhere whispers, "Hey, you!"

Ghosts here are seen as well as heard. Five luminescent specters float in a group down the passageways. A visually repugnant phantom that comes out at night is sometimes described as having a burned face and sometimes as having a blood-covered face. A security guard in 1993 reported just such an encounter; the apparition's facial skin and tattered clothes were severely burned, and it was hovering in the air, advancing without touching the deck. The employee quit his job in a hurry.

Perhaps a clue is to be gleaned from the ship's picture gallery, where portraits of each of the Sullivan brothers hang in a row. Ordinary camera wielding can yield unsettling paranormal results here, for attempts to photograph this wall of portraiture are thwarted by glowing white spots that block the face of George Sullivan. Why does his image stand out with such ghostly uniqueness? Perhaps it is because he was the last to depart the earthly realm, and only after having searched fruitlessly for the others. They had preceded him in death; but in the end, of course, he did join up with them. They stuck together. They stick together still.

A Hornet's Nest of Hauntings

The day-to-day risks inherent in warship service are an open-ended invitation to the paranormal. If sailors are a notoriously superstitious lot, it is because their lives are notoriously dangerous. For what is superstition but an encoded form of self-preservation? A keyed-up sensitivity to cause and effect, to caution and portent, comes naturally to those constantly on the edge of hazardous duty and perilous circumstance. Whether amid the storm of battle or in the normal flow of routine in calmer seas, the fighting-ship sailor is acutely aware that any watch might be the one when the Reaper comes calling.

The USS *Hornet*, an aircraft carrier preserved for public visitation at Alameda, California, is a salient example of a high-risk working environment layered with the supernatural reverberations of mishap and trauma. Fifty-nine times she was attacked, yet not a single Japanese torpedo, bomb, or kamikaze ever found its mark. No, in war she remained unscarred. Some 270–300 sailors died aboard the *Hornet* nevertheless during her twenty-seven years of naval service, and the ship has come under the intensive scrutiny of paranormalist investigation teams in the wake of a stunning and escalating number of ghost sightings. The *Hornet*, it seems, is a veritable hornet's nest of hauntings.

Like her *Essex*-class sisters (and sister ghost ships) the *Lexington* and *Yorktown*, the *Hornet* was named for an earlier carrier lost in the first years of World War II. The previous *Hornet* had gained fame in the Doolittle raid and the Battle of Midway before being sunk during the Battle of the Santa Cruz Islands in October 1942. The next ship to perpetuate the *Hornet* name (a name gracing Navy ships all the way back to the Revolutionary War) was launched and commissioned in late 1943 and was in the Pacific action by June 1944 bombing Saipan and Tinian, Rota and Guam. She unleashed the opening raids of the Battle of the Philippine

Sea, contributed to the resounding success of the Marianas Turkey Shoot, supported the landings at Leyte, and helped sink an entire Japanese convoy at Ormoc Bay. She was there for Iwo Jima and Okinawa, and she scored the initial hits in the sinking of the mighty *Yamato*. In all, the *Hornet*'s planes sank more than 1,269,000 tons of Japanese shipping and wreaked concomitant havoc on Japan's air wing. In the process of destroying 1,410 Japanese aircraft, the *Hornet* set World War II's record for the most enemy planes downed in a single day: 67. And in a karmic nod to her namesake predecessor, the *Hornet*'s flyers were the first to hit Tokyo since the previous *Hornet*'s 1942 Doolittle raid. In the 1950s and 1960s the *Hornet* became a staple of the Seventh Fleet, operating from Vietnam to Japan. And before her 1970 decommissioning she had the honor of being the retrieval ship for the 1969 splashdown of *Apollo 11*, welcoming back to Earth the first men on the Moon.

But even a vessel as successful and highly decorated as the *Hornet* has her dark side. An aircraft carrier is, after all, an inordinately dangerous place to work. And in addition to her requisite share of deaths by propeller blades, jet intakes, burning ordnance, flailing flight cables, and the violence that can erupt between men under duress, the *Hornet* also somehow managed to garner the negative distinction of having the highest suicide rate of any ship in the history of the U.S. Navy. The evanescent remnants of endings tragic and untimely have accrued throughout the *Hornet*'s vast, intricate superstructure; weird manifestations were jarring crewmen by at least as early as the 1960s. And when the ship was rescued from mothballs in 1995 and a new generation of restorers, caretakers, and visitors came to occupy her decks, abundant ghosts were roused anew.

The headless corpse that lurches back and forth across the catapult room has terrified witnesses to the very threshold of madness. Many say that the sighting of this grotesque figure is the single most horrible experience in a lifetime. If an aircraft carrier is one of the most hazardous workplaces in the world, then the catapult room is one of the most hazardous workplaces on an aircraft carrier. Here, where ingenious machinery imparts instantaneous lift-off velocity to planes, flinging them off the flight deck and into the air, the cable wires instrumental to the process are occasionally susceptible to snapping. A snapped cable is like a razor-sharp serpent spinning lethally at five hundred miles per hour, slashing and slicing everything in its path indiscriminately. At least three of the *Hornet*'s crewmen are known to have been decapitated in this manner; one of them remains, haunting the catapult room, doomed to grope in search of his missing head for a wretched eternity.

The engine room necessary to power a behemoth warship is another location with high potential for fatal misfortune. In clattering confines where 1,500-degree steam courses at high pressure through keening pipes, the room temperature can rise past 125 degrees even when all is well. Add a ruptured pipe to this powder keg, and lethality of the most gruesome sort ensues. A pitiable, gore-soaked monster of a ghost appears as vivid and nauseating testimony to one such tragedy, and has been a recurrent presence on the *Hornet* since the Vietnam era. In life he was a sailor whose arm was cut off by the laser-like effluence of concentrated heat jetting forth from a broken pipe. He was found later by his shipmates, who were aghast at the realization that his blood literally had boiled, causing his skin to peel away like a scorched and lacerated fruit rind. He hovers about the master control panel to this day, a fearsome sight. A witness who saw him in 2008 described his "uniform matted with glistening blood, his burned flesh hung in grotesque ribbons from his bones, eyeballs bulging in stark terror." When the burn-victim phantom suddenly disappears, he leaves behind the acrid stench of cooked viscera.

A sad specter who met a similar fate haunts the *Hornet*'s sick bay. He was a sailor who lost his footing on the flight deck and slipped right into the path of a landing aircraft. The propeller sheared off the top of his head and laid bare his brain while the intense heat of the jet's engine incinerated his uniform and torched his body. Barely alive, he was rushed to the sick-bay operating table where he died within moments. But perhaps because of the instant and traumatic exposure of his brain matter to the elements, he became locked in that vile moment and never realized he was dead. And so his spirit essence remains in sick bay to this day, a residual entity with a sense of self-identity retained past death's brink. A psychic accurately described the details of the sailor's deadly accident with no prior knowledge of the occurrence—aware of what happened because of the ghost's powerful presence.

On a ship with a crew numbering in the thousands, unfortunate incidents of an interpersonal nature also are likely to transpire. Even a convivial mess hall can be the stage for a drama with an unhappy ending, thus becoming another shipboard site haunted by the legacy of foul moments. Infrared cameras in 2001 captured the image of the legendary *Hornet* mess hall ghost and helped verify stories of a long-ago chow-line murder.

The luckless victim, impatiently standing in line with rumbling stomach, bumped into the crewman in front of him. The contact led to heated words between men grouchy with hunger. Words led to shoves, and shoves led to flying fists. The accidental instigator of the donnybrook quickly found himself surrounded by his antagonist's friends, who proceeded to pound him to a pulp. In the heat of the moment they beat him to death. And his ghost has been a cafeteria presence ever since, his appetite never sated, his life never completed, his indignity at his unfair killing never fading. He is, in effect, a prisoner of the mess hall.

A far surlier prisoner can be found just where one might expect: namely, the brig. A distinctly hostile force is incarcerated in the brig of the *Hornet*, unseen yet felt, invisible yet violent. Here, among a shipload of American ghosts, is a Japanese ghost, and an enraged one at that. In the waning weeks of World War II a kamikaze failed in its attempt to crash into the *Hornet*, plummeting instead into the water alongside. The pilot was rescued and placed behind bars on the *Hornet*. Thwarted in his mission to sacrifice himself in a blaze of glory for Japan, the pilot went insane. He finally managed to defy the efforts of his captors to keep him alive and succeeded in committing suicide in the brig, casting an enduring spell of powerful malevolence on the spot. During the *Hornet*'s years of active service, sailors who were tossed in the brig would afterward tell disbelieving superiors that an invisible entity attacked them as they tried to sleep. In the carrier's current incarnation as a museum ship, psychics have ventured into the brig and reported that the kamikaze ghost is "extremely powerful" and "angry." One overnight visitor made the nearly fatal error of going on a midnight ramble that led him deep into the ship's recesses; the further below he ventured, the more lost he became. He stumbled at last onto a place with cots. Huffing and sweating, he was gratified to find a welcoming mattress on which to catch his breath before attempting the long maze quest back topside. So glad, in fact, that he didn't mind the jail bars that told him this was the old brig. He nodded off with ease but awoke, he later said, "feeling as if someone was violently choking me! Jumping off the cot, I had the distinct impression someone had his hands clasped around my throat." He managed to break free from the phantom's strangling grasp, let out a garbled scream, and "dashed down the passageway as fast as my legs would move. . . . That incident put an end to my lone explorations of *Hornet*'s labyrinth of corridors."

Many others on the *Hornet* have felt the creepy touch of invisible hands. A sailor who served aboard her was yanked out of his bunk and pulled to the floor multiple times by a forceful and determined (and invisible) spirit. Visitors have reported tactile disturbances that range from the feeling of being brushed up against, to a sharp and unmistakable tap on the shoulder, to being grabbed, pushed, beaten, or slapped on the back of the head. A woman endured the revulsion of having a ghost walk right through her body. And a worker helping to renovate the ship was hospitalized after being plowed into a bulkhead by an angry entity. "You've got a giant steel cocoon formerly inhabited by thousands of men of different temperaments over a period of nearly 30 years," said Bob Messiah, a *Hornet* docent and former crew member. "Things happened. Tempers ignited. . . . Trouble ensued and grew intense enough to invade the spirit world."

Others, while not physically violated, have been bowled over by the paranoid sensation of spectral proximity, of being voyeurized by long-dead eyes. A TV news reporter who braved a shipboard overnighter found herself the unwanted target of such eerie attention. "I could have sworn someone else was beside me," she recounted. " I could 'feel' its chilling nearness . . . and hear its breathing. . . . I kept shuddering, unable to shake the feeling an unseen presence was beside me in that cabin." Her experience was not unique. "I got the strong feeling that I wasn't alone," recalled another visitor, "that same type of feeling you get when somebody gets inside your personal space. The hairs on the back of my neck stood up and I got goose pimples on my forearms . . . somebody, something was moving toward me or perhaps circling around me."

The officers' berth is imbued with such a profoundly negative presence that psychics have learned to steer clear. Some of those who did try to enter were wracked by the extrasensory echoes of "unspeakable cruelty and suffering" and felt a strong pushing against their chests keeping them out. Glowing clusters of ghost lights often appear here, while a "deep blue amoeba-like plasma" has been seen on the fo'c'sle. Such visual anomalies also show up on tourists' videotapes; when the film is played back in slow motion, ethereal blobs of light become more sharply defined as a striped sleeve, a hand, a pack of cigarettes rolled up in the arm of a T-shirt—traces of human forms that are merely brief flashes to the naked eye.

Violence, suicide, and grisly accidents all cast their ghostly pall on the *Hornet*, and some two hundred paranormal experiences were reported within the first four years of the ship's reawakening in 1995. So prevalent were the incidents that the *Hornet*'s staff felt compelled to summon experts trained in the burgeoning science of ghost detection. The Office of Paranormal Investigations (OPI) arrived in 1999 to record and cross-reference interviews, investigate the phenomena-rich portions of the ship, and document their findings. "The experiences aboard the *Hornet* are intriguing for a number of reasons," said OPI parapsychologist Loyd Auerbach. "First of all, the witnesses themselves, for the most part, are people with little or no paranormal experience. Some skeptics have changed their tune after the experiences."

Auerbach and San Francisco–based psychic Stache Margaret Murray interviewed more than thirty witnesses—*Hornet* Foundation members, museum staff, restoration workers, volunteers, maintenance men, and security guards—and Auerbach soon concluded that the *Hornet* comprises "what may be one of the most fascinating ghost investigations" of his life.

In addition to the sheer volume of incidents, there was a better than usual degree of veracity among the reports. "There are a number of multiple witness sightings," reported Auerbach. "Having more than one witness to the same event provides us not only with more than one viewpoint, but also some degree of corroboration that the event was more than purely subjective."

As OPI workers sifted through the massive and mounting empirical data, a remarkable possibility began to emerge: the *Hornet* hauntings seem to separate out into categorical layers. There are, of course, the numerous disturbed (and disturbing) ghosts who are locked into the vectors of their sudden and violent deaths. But Murray and other psychics believe that additional spirits are gathering there as well, "cohesive and positive" spirits, the vestiges of sailors going about their business—"people," summarized Auerbach, "who did serve on the U.S.S. *Hornet* at one time, but did not necessarily die anywhere near the ship."

In 1999, Alan McKean, a charter member of the *Hornet* Foundation, was giving a ship's tour to a group representing a potential corporate sponsor. They were on the flag bridge when McKean "looked over and saw a fellow in khakis . . . going down the ladder." The old-fashioned uniform appeared to be that of a senior officer. "He turned around and looked over his left shoulder directly at me. . . . He didn't say a word. Then he went down the ladder." One of the touring executives also saw the mystery figure. McKean sped down the ladder in pursuit, but the khaki-clad wraith had vanished.

"It wasn't scary," said McKean. "It wasn't a cold look he gave me. Just very businesslike."

Another of the Foundation's charter members, Bob Rogers, had a similar encounter in 1999. While descending to main control, he said, "I could see someone in a khaki uniform going down the ladder below me." Rogers followed the figure down to the engineering area, but "no one was there. That's a confined space. . . . I went in the main and only entrance to that space that was open. The other side was locked up and chained closed."

Rogers described the figure as dark-haired and seemingly focused on some mission; he didn't acknowledge Rogers coming down the ladder right behind him. "The escape route was locked. No one was in there. There's no way someone could have gotten by me."

Hornet staffer Dorothy Tallmadge also had a run-in with a non-communicative ghost in uniform. She encountered him while en route to the flight mess lounge. "It was a man, wearing khaki." Talmadge said hello, went on her way, and then sensed something weird about the run-in. "I thought, wait a minute. He made no response to me. He didn't say anything. He just stared. I saw him full front just standing there, still, arms to his side." She dashed back. The stranger had merged back into the shadows whence he came.

As Yuletide approached in 1998, two *Hornet* staffers were adorning one of the hangar bays with a tall Christmas tree when a sailor wearing a Navy pea coat over his uniform appeared and ran straight into (and through) the tree. "We walked all around the perimeter of the tree, and no one was there," recalled Keith LaDue. "No one was there!" The pea-coated figure had continued on his course, impervious to his witnesses and to such obstacles as a fifteen-foot tree in his predetermined path.

A similarly impervious ghost, unaware of his observers and concentrating on the task at hand, appears when the proper mixture of environmental factors dovetail: it must be the night of a full moon, but it must be cloudy as well. Then he shows himself, a tall pilot in helmet and goggles walking determinedly along the flight deck's center line, replaying forever his preparatory steps toward some long-forgotten sortie.

The uniformed, businesslike ghost crew of the *Hornet* is not merely a recently discovered phenomenon. Just prior to her decommissioning in

1970, a number of witnesses reported seeing a pipe-smoking officer in a World War II–period khaki uniform at the entrance to the hangar deck elevator. The strong aroma of pipe tobacco preceded the officer's appearance, and after he was spotted he instantly disappeared.

While the majority of sightings involving ghosts in uniform have been noninteractive, exchanges do sometimes occur between apparitions and humans. An overnight visitor was lying in his bunk when a sailor appeared out of nowhere, said, "I used to sleep there," then dissolved back into nothingness. And one night, as Keith LaDue continued laboring past the time when anyone else was aboard the ship, he was alarmed to hear the chattering voices of plane crews "talking shop, dropping tools, and working on airplanes, talking about the airplanes they were working on, and parts, and home." LaDue, determined to finish his task, entreated them to quiet down long enough for him to complete his work and get out of their midst. And they apparently heard and heeded him, for no sooner had he asked than their banter suddenly ceased.

Between fearful spirits trapped by tragic demise and a hustling, bustling complement of long-dead, still-working officers and men, the *Hornet* is indeed swarming with spirit activity. "Two things could be going on," theorized Auerbach. In one of the haunting categories, "there's no interaction, no recognition. It's like someone looking at you from out of a TV set. You can't engage them." Then there are more the clear-cut "apparition cases," paranormal situations that are "more interactive. Someone has stuck around after death. The person may have unfinished business."

In between the two haunting extremes is a shadowy area that paranormal research is still on the fringes of grasping. Regardless of other spectral causes, a difficult-to-pinpoint environmental factor may be involved as well. "Something in the environment at the time of death allows that person to stick around," Auerbach explained. "Magnetic fields, geomagnetic fields, the position of the earth—there are a whole bunch of things we're looking at right now."

In ghost-rich environments such as that of the *Hornet*, the pioneers of paranormal research are probing ever further toward some sense of how our dimension and the dimension of the dead overlap, advancing to the place where physics melds into metaphysics, where the people from an earlier era see us just as we are seeing them, our moment and theirs somehow folding into one another. "In effect," mused Auerbach, "we're piercing the veil of time."

To the ghosts, it is their ship and we are the intruders. Perhaps we are a frightening sight and they tell each other hushed and spooky stories about us. Perhaps some of them comfort themselves by contending that we are the product of some dead sailor's overactive imagination, and that we don't really exist.

How dare they?

Of Hangars and Their Hangers-On

The tale was told among the sailors of the *Hornet* that whenever she was at sea, a ghostly formation of aircraft could be seen following the carrier's wake at twilight. But they were not the *Hornet*'s planes—not this *Hornet*, anyway. They came from the previous *Hornet* that had sunk in 1942, and they were doomed to fly forever in vain pursuit of the ship's flight deck. They were the fifteen planes of Torpedo Squadron 8 that had been shot down at the Battle of Midway during a gallant but doomed attack, a lost squadron offering a twilight reminder that just as airpower became a key component of sea power in the twentieth century, so too has the Navy's pantheon of ghosts come to include those of the airborne variety. And from one end of the country to the other, airfields and hangars at present and former Navy locations are imbued with the haunting mystique of phantom planes, phantom flyers, and fiery finales.

It seems fitting that the place often fondly referred to as "the Annapolis of the Air" would be home to a resident spectral flying ace. But it is worth noting that Florida's Pensacola Naval Air Station is, in fact, steeped in history (and hauntings). The Navy's presence at the site far predates the station's emergence as one of the world's premier flight-training centers. The Pensacola Naval Hospital opened in 1826, and the Navy yard there was well established by the time the Confederates commandeered it during the Civil War. The Pensacola naval story lies in layers like an archaeological dig, and the ghosts rise up teeming from different chapters of the saga, merging in a macabre masquerade ball of disparate styles and customs. Eerily glowing figures drift down stairways of buildings in use since the nineteenth century. Objects fly across rooms. Baleful inscriptions suddenly deface walls. "Help, Let Me Out!" and "Death Awaits!" are among the horrifying communications scrawled by some netherworld hand. Faded voices from the yellow fever epidemic of the 1880s emanate from the dark depths of the hospital, and a keeper who perished on the job continues to haunt the Pensacola Lighthouse. A plaintive widow from the Civil War remains as a phosphorescent white evanescence in Quarters A, where the ghost of Commodore Woolsey, an eccentric commandant whose ardor for medicinal spiced rum failed to prevent his death by yellow fever, continues to pace the cupola at night.

But with due deference to the station's rich history, to the general populace the name "Pensacola" connotes Navy "flight school," an association it has been earning since the earliest days of the naval aviation concept. During World War I Pensacola became one of the Navy's first full-time air stations, and more airfields, more facilities, and more personnel continued to be added in the 1920s. In this period of a rapidly expanding aviation program, the oldest intact building on the original Navy yard came to be used as flight officers' quarters. The 1834 octagonal structure directly across from the haunted commandant's house had been many things in its time; its role as a chapel spared it from destruction by the retreating Confederates in 1862. And as naval aviation started coming of age, the old octagon became home to the fearless and talented new breed of flying men.

Capt. Guy B. Hall, USMC, embodied the romanticized image of the dashing pilot that captured the imagination of the early-twentieth-century public, a devil-may-care spirit and rugged good looks encased in a leather jacket and tall boots. He had a ready smile, an educated taste in whiskey, and a gambler's soul that appreciated the pleasures of an all-night poker session when not savoring the exhilarating perils of flying. Flight is inherently a high-stakes, high-risk proposition; in the fragile bi-winged planes with open cockpits of the 1920s it was all the more so. The captain was assigned to Pensacola as a flight instructor, as worthy a duty for a gambler as there could be. Even when one was ace-quality skilled, the dangers were constant and immediate. Two Voight airplanes flown by Marine lieutenants were tossed like dry leaves by strong wind gusts and crashed into each other three thousand feet over Pensacola in 1923, a deadly reminder of the tenuousness of planes and pilots alike. When he wasn't braving such everyday threats as a routine part of his job, Captain Hall held court at epic poker games in his octagon quarters. Any card player who sat in with him soon learned the captain's trademark quirk, his habit of picking up his poker chips and idly letting them drop back on the table, generating a distinct and resonant clacking.

Captain Hall, one of those who set the swashbuckling standard for all who since have followed them skyward, was killed in a failed landing attempt on Corry Field in 1926, his death a sad testament to the fact that even the good do not fly risk-free. The old octagonal building that was his temporary residence at Pensacola is today known as Building 16 and is the home of the Navy–Marine Corps Trial Judiciary's Trial Service Office. And to this day it is haunted by the poker-playing ghost. The falling poker chips of Captain Hall still resound with their clackety-clack rhythm through Building 16, where a flyer's all-night poker game has transmogrified into an eternal one.

Eight hundred and ninety-one miles inland from Pensacola, a naval air station arose hastily on the Kansas prairie to meet the exigencies of World War II and continued to train flyers up through the Vietnam era. The Olathe Naval Air Station is no more; in the 1970s it was converted into the Johnson County Industrial Airport, which in turn subsequently metamorphosed into the New Century Air Center. But vestiges of its naval origins remain, paranormal traces of the thirty-four fatalities that occurred on the site during its years as a Navy flight-training base. Much of its supernatural legendry centers on the infamous Hangar 43, but that is not the sole spectral spot; this haunted heartland facility has plenty of ghostly residents elsewhere.

Commissioned in 1942, the Olathe Naval Air Station quickly became a beehive; some 4,500 naval cadets trained there in World War II alone. Three gigantic hangars were built with two-hundred-foot bays on each side. One of these unprecedentedly large wooden structures, Hangar 43, would remain standing and in use almost to the end of the century. Over the years, mechanics, guards, and others working there offered disturbing testimony of a whistling ghost that walked the catwalk overhead. The hangar phantom slammed doors in people's faces, upended coffee cups, turned on faucets, and always seemed to return to his default pastime: parading on the catwalk whistling eerie melodies. "I don't want anyone to know I believe in ghosts," a worker told the *Kansas City Business Journal* on the condition of anonymity, "but this hangar is definitely haunted."

A witness may actually have sighted the usually invisible whistler one night after midnight. The ethereal figure was described as "a person dressed in white, like a military uniform." Was this the selfsame musical ghost or a different presence entirely? The spirit, or spirits, of Hangar 43 continue to haunt the modern airport that has come to occupy the space, and whether it is a single ghost or many, a nickname collects them all into one entity, "the Commander," and associates him with one of the fatal plane crashes that occurred at Olathe Naval Air Station.

But the crash most often linked to the Hangar 43 hauntings has no immediately apparent direct connection to the hangar. An Army pilot, Lt. Neal R. Webster, tried to come in for an emergency landing at Olathe and careened into the administration building on January 3, 1949, at 5 AM. Webster was killed. His passenger, Pvt. Thomas Ruse of Lowery Air Force Base in Denver, lived long enough to be rushed to the station's sick bay but died later that morning after briefly regaining consciousness. Oddly, an eyewitness to the crash claimed to have seen a passenger walk away from the wreckage and then mysteriously disappear.

Paranormal events soon followed this mishap; the administration building and its environs began to exhibit strange occurrences. Through the years, the ghostly manifestations of the 1949 crash merged in memory with the discrete hauntings of Hangar 43 (many erroneous accounts describe the plane as having crashed into the hangar). But these are separate ghosts entirely. Several people are known to have fallen to their death from the treacherous heights of Hangar 43, affording ample opportunities for site-specific spirits. Other parts of Olathe were known to be haunted as well—the long-ago demolished Hangar 21, for example. (The sick bay, too, would have had its share.) Hangar 43 may have had some connection to one of Olathe's other fatal crashes, but not the crash of 1949—that tragedy involved soldiers in transit, while, judging from his uniform, the Hangar 43 ghost was a Navy man.

Fifteen hundred and eighty-four miles west by southwest of Olathe, Kansas, amid the sprawling naval complex of San Diego, California, a hangar still bears the imprints, both concrete and psychic, of a calamitous accident that filled the air with smoke, flame, shrapnel, and screams in 1969. Officials declared the incident at Miramar Naval Air Station "the worst disaster in San Diego County history." The results of that fateful morning would have been all the more tragic, however, and the death toll considerably higher, had it not been for the unhesitating heroism of the sailors who rallied to rescue their comrades from the sudden and all-consuming conflagration. Some were beyond saving, killed instantly in the roaring blaze and deafening explosions that marked this spot for all time as a grim Miramar landmark: haunted Hangar 1.

Four Navy F-8 Crusader jets of Fighter Squadron 194 took off from Miramar at 9:55 AM on December 22, 1969, for routine maneuvers over the Pacific Ocean. Several minutes later, about forty miles out at sea, one of the F-8 pilots, a Navy lieutenant who had recently served a tour of duty in Vietnam aboard the carrier USS *Oriskany*, radioed in that his oil pressure was dangerously low and that he was flying back to base immediately. Descending from an altitude of one thousand feet for an emergency landing, the lieutenant was at four hundred feet and about a quarter of a mile from the Miramar runway when a series of internal explosions rocked his jet. The oil pressure continued to plummet, and the lieutenant ejected from the cockpit. As his parachute billowed open and he drifted to the ground near U.S. Route 395, the now-pilotless jet rocketed toward the air station.

A machinist's mate on duty at Hangar 1 that morning remembered looking up and seeing the rogue F-8 right before it hit. For a brief moment of suspended time, the jet "sort of floated in the air." And then the world became one big fireball.

At 10:31 AM the 45,000-pound supersonic jet crashed through the partially closed bay doors of Hangar 1 at a speed of 250 miles per hour. About sixty people were in the hangar as the jet skidded under two parked F-4 Phantoms and exploded. "It felt as though somebody had lifted me by the seat of my pants," a chief petty officer said. "The force of the explosion was that great." Jet fuel and oxygen tanks combusted in exponential escalation of the initial burst as planes were blown to bits and fire rolled like gathering thunder. "It was like shrapnel and napalm flying around," said a witness. As one of the jets exploded, its ejection mechanism activated and the seat torpedoed through the hangar roof. Manhole covers ripped free and popped upward in the percussive shock. Some men managed to evacuate. Some were incinerated instantly. Some were knocked out by the blast and trapped inside by walls of flame.

"The aircraft could not have hit at a worse place," Miramar Fire Chief William Knight said. "Not only was there a congestion of personnel in the area, but also there were numerous aircraft fully loaded with fuel."

The surviving sailors shook off their initial shock and immediately began rescue operations. "If it wasn't for the way those guys went to work despite the possibility of more explosions, it could have been a hell of a lot worse and there could have been a hell of a lot more dead," said Lt. Cdr. David Burleigh, who had been in a nearby hangar when the disaster struck. Fire Chief Knight echoed his sentiments. "Instead of running from the hangar, men were running into it, pulling out the wounded, carrying out their buddies. It took more than guts to go in there. They charged into the face of secondary explosions and fire. The men disregarded their own personal safety, and in so doing averted what could have been an even worse disaster."

Nine men were killed in the hangar and two more had died by the next morning; twelve others were injured. Three F-8 Crusaders docked in the hangar were severely damaged, and five F-4 Phantoms were utterly destroyed. Total damages were estimated at $25 million. But the incalculable cost always comes down to the lives lost. The eleven killed in the Hangar 1 tragedy included a pair of young brothers serving as aircraft mechanics and a forty-one-year-old chief weapons officer who had just narrowly escaped death in a fire aboard the USS *Enterprise* the previous January; a veteran chief petty officer who was one year away from retirement and an air fuel controller technician married for a mere six months. Hundreds gathered for a service at the Miramar Naval Air Station's Airman Memorial Chapel. Wives, daughters, sons, and friends wept uncontrollably as light filtered down through frosted windows onto the Christmas tree and poinsettias that had been put in the chapel to celebrate the season. Three days before Christmas, their worlds all had been shattered.

The Miramar Naval Air Station is Marine Corps Air Station Miramar now, but Hangar 1 remains, along with what one witness described as the hangar's "non-corporeal inhabitants." They have been a well-known factor of Hangar 1 duty since the 1970s. Shadowy forms, opaque and human shaped, walk the long corridors. They hover outside doorways, peering through the glass, knocking on the door, then vanishing when approached, leaving one staring down a long, empty hallway with an unshakeable sense of dread. Like the visible fissures that still scar the wall as a reminder of the 1969 tragedy, the ghosts that haunt Hangar 1 are inseparable from the fabric of the structure; it belongs to them by death right.

That they are not more numerous is testament to the courage of the sailors who ventured back into the fire, risking death in order to snatch others from its jaws. Their heroism came not during the adrenalized fury of battle but on a calm Monday morning turned hellish in the blink of an eye. And it was in just such a fiery scenario—one of unforetold happenstance, of disaster, flames, and young sailors rising to the unexpected urgencies of the moment—that one of the most troublesome hauntings in modern naval history was spawned.

Hell's Flight Deck

She was the largest, mightiest, most futuristic aircraft carrier ever built. When the USS *Forrestal* was launched in December 1954, the age of the supercarrier was launched along with her. She was the avatar of the new class, dwarfing her World War II forebears in firepower, fuel capacity, speed, and sheer size. All of the lessons that had been learned in carrier design had been incorporated into her creation, and the 1,046-foot *Forrestal* was the embodiment of many firsts: the first carrier built specifically with jet aircraft in mind and the first to launch with an angled flight deck (with which older carriers were then being refitted), steam catapults, landing lights, nuclear-payload capabilities, air-conditioned quarters—the list goes on. Her very presence symbolized America's power and global reach. The supership was named for FDR's secretary of the Navy (and the first-ever secretary of defense), James V. Forrestal, who committed suicide in 1949 by jumping from a sixteenth-story window at the Bethesda Naval Hospital (though conspiracy-minded historians to this day suspect foul play). It has been said that the *Forrestal* was to aircraft carriers what HMS *Dreadnought* had been to battleships—the apotheosis of a type. Another comparison might be to say that the *Forrestal* was to aircraft carriers what the *Titanic* had been to ocean liners.

For twelve years the *Forrestal* went to sea on numerous show-the-flag missions and served as an important springboard for naval technology experimentation, but she had yet to be deployed for actual combat. The Vietnam War provided the opportunity, and in June 1967 she departed Norfolk for the Tonkin Gulf, where she would help step up the aerial assault on the enemy headquartered at Hanoi. By July 25 she was on Yankee Station in the waters off North Vietnam and enjoined with other ships in Aircraft Carrier Air Wing 17 in launching multiple daily bombing raids in heavy rotation. The group flew 150 bomb-delivering missions in four days. Running short of good modern bombs, the *Forrestal* was forced to accept decrepit old World War II–vintage Composition B bombs from the supply ship.

The *Forrestal* was preparing to let fly the morning's second wave of strikes on July 29 when a power surge unleashed a 5-inch rocket from the pod of an F-4 Phantom II parked on the starboard stern. The rocket shot across the deck and struck a wing-mounted fuel tank on an A-4 Skyhawk waiting to launch. Fuel spurted like arterial blood and the flight deck erupted in flames. Pilots lined up for takeoff were cooked in their cockpits, and each plane that burned fed more fuel to the fire, begetting an ever-higher mountain of flames and black smoke. Bombs were heating to the bursting point as the fire emergency crew rushed to contain them. But because they were the volatile, more heat-sensitive old hand-me-down Composition B bombs, the firefighters had less time, and the old bombs exploded, taking out the all-important fire team within the first two minutes of the catastrophe.

A future senator and presidential candidate named Lt. Cdr. John McCain leapt from his A-4 cockpit and climbed down the nose of his burning plane with all the speed he could muster, clearing it just before its bombs fell to the deck and exploded. Other A-4s in the line burned and blew up in the escalating chain reaction, and great gaping craters cracked open in the rupturing flight deck. Fire shot down through lower decks, incinerating sailors in their quarters and trapping men behind walls of flame and deadly smoke. More and more Composition B bombs exploded, and the smoke-choked air was alive with shrapnel as jet fuel continued to spread across the deck like a widening lake of fire. For sixteen hours the exhausted crew battled the flames that dominated topside and coursed through the ship's lower reaches. When it all was over, 134 sailors were dead and 161 were severely injured. The *Forrestal* had come perilously close to sinking and had suffered $72 million worth of damage—the most powerful, most modern aircraft carrier in the world laid low by a combination of second-rate, out-of-date bombs and plain bad luck.

The *Forrestal* fire was one of the worst accidents in U.S. naval history, and the ship sustained the worst loss of life on a U.S. Navy vessel since World War II. Seven months' worth of repairs would have the *Forrestal* ready again for action, but her role in the Vietnam War had ended, curtailed after four and a half days. The mighty supercarrier would spend the rest of her career on Mediterranean and Indian Ocean deployments and

stationed at various eastern seaboard ports. Fire-prevention training vid-
eos of the tragedy became required viewing throughout the fleet. Others
might apply mordant and disparaging nicknames to her—the USS *Forrest
Fire*, the USS *Firestal*—but those who served on her still referred to her
proudly by her more positive moniker, "the Mighty FID" (the acronym
indicating "First in Defense," as in the ship's namesake and the slogan
on her insignia patch). And whenever two veterans of service aboard the
Mighty FID chanced to run into each other somewhere, a standard remark
would be, "So I wonder how old George is these days."

All *Forrestal* sailors knew who George was.

"George" is as serviceable and innocuously pleasant a name as any for
a ship's resident ghost, but as is often the case with a highly haunted vessel,
the designation undoubtedly is a convenient umbrella for numerous spirits.
That the *Forrestal* carried abundant spectral presences is understandable.
Even a skeptic would be hard-pressed not to feel an unpleasant chill putting head to pillow in berthing quarters where many sailors were incinerated in their bunks. The ghostly pall hangs heavy in this area below the
flight deck, where squadron members in the post-1967 era continued to be
assigned to sleep (or try to sleep). "I would hear voices in the night crying
for help," an air wing crewman recalled of his 1982 stay in the haunted
berth. "On numerous occasions I would see a sailor . . . walk into an area
that was just a plain old bulkhead. He would completely disappear."

Here and in other belowdecks spaces on the *Forrestal* where fires had
raced through from the flame-engulfed flight deck, ghostly sightings were
common. Strange noises, doors locking and unlocking, the clasping grip of
invisible hands—reports of such strange doings were rife; more often than
not the phenomena were accompanied by the fleeting glimpse of a man
in khaki. And sometimes, those who got more than a passing look at the
elusive figure wished they hadn't, for what remained of his face appeared
to have "melted features."

By 1988, some sailors were flatly disobeying direct orders to proceed
into certain parts of the ship, more terrified of what lurked there than they
were of officers' punitive measures. Central to their fears was a storage area
that had once been the morgue. "I've got one guy working for me . . . who
refuses to go down there alone," P.O. Daniel Balboa reported. "Our last
chief petty officer in charge, who has since transferred, refused to go down
there at all."

P.O. James Hillard was one of those who ventured into the ghostly zones and emerged with the adamant conviction that he would never go down there again. Curious about the source of strange footsteps he was hearing, he went to investigate and found himself fast on the heels of an apparition. "He was wearing a khaki uniform, like an officer or chief would wear." Hillard pursued the phantom into a dead-end hold, but "there was nobody in there, and I swear that's where he went." Another crewman watched a khaki-clad wraith descending a ladder, and it is probably for the best that the crewman did not follow; the hunter might have found himself the hunted. For it was in just such a ladder-sharing situation that a sailor was grabbed by his legs so tightly, by something powerful yet unseen, that one of his shipmates had to tug desperately to pull him free.

In 1993, after the *Forrestal* was decommissioned and laid up in the Philadelphia Navy Yard, a welder was dismantling food storage equipment when he started hearing a loud clanging. The welder grabbed a wrench and returned the clang signal. After a pause, his clangs were answered by more clangs. Curious now, he investigated the source of the communication, and experienced an electric jolt of terror when he saw "a chief petty officer horribly burned just staring at me. And then he slowly fades away. . . . Needless to say I got out of there real fast!"

That last reported ghost sighting on the *Forrestal* to date was graphic, gruesome, the stuff of nightmares. But perhaps the most heart-rending and bizarre paranormal manifestation on the supercarrier was experienced, again, by Petty Officer Hillard. It started with the peal of a telephone. "The phone rang and I answered it. . . . There was a faint voice calling, 'Help! Help! I'm on the sixth deck!'"

The strangest thing about the plaintive call?

It came in on a phone that was disconnected.

Desperate hands groping for a lifeline; scurrying, sadly disfigured officer ghosts; earnest pleas for help from a voice trapped in a time and place where no help can come—the nature of the *Forrestal*'s ghosts bespeak tragedy of a historic degree. In raging fire on the Tonkin Gulf, 134 sailors joined the eternal crew, a crew whose roll call will continue to grow as long as there are ships and seas and stalwart souls yearning for the horizon.

For Those in Peril on the Sea

From the days of canvas, cutlass, and cannon to the days of reactors, jets, and missiles, they have haunted the wide waves—an unbroken continuum of phantom ships and phantom crews, sailing down through the ages with the spectral tide. For naval history has always had a supernatural subtext, a logic-defying yet intuitively knowable undercurrent as tangible as the mystique of the ocean on a moonlit night. The fleeting jolts of the paranormal that can occur in a sailor's life beckon with the dark promise of an inner truth above and beyond the dry chronicle of human events. Like a sudden lightning flash illuminating a black nocturnal gale for a brief second before darkness reenvelops the world, a supernatural manifestation offers a tantalizing and all-too-brief glimpse of realities normally unseeable. In some ancient way, the sea and the spirit world intertwine; all who venture across the waves know it to be so. Some deny it; some scoff; but all, inside, know it.

When a spectral visitation does occur, such metaphysical ruminations become moot; what was felt to be possible suddenly becomes frighteningly palpable. During World War II a young woman awoke to find her boyfriend standing by her bed. He was supposed to be overseas, serving in the Navy. A subtle glow outlined his form as he tried to say something, finally giving up and vanishing. The woman subsequently found out that he had been killed by a kamikaze off Okinawa—killed at the same time that he was visiting her bedside. How can science rectify such an occurrence with its strict rules of the concrete and the logical? An officer on a Navy cruiser awoke to find himself staring into the blurred face of a floating body. Later, looking in a cruise book, he found a memorial page dedicated to a petty officer who had been killed by electrocution. The face on that page was the same face that had appeared before him in his stateroom, and the death had transpired two decks above in a spot directly over his rack. How can the laws of reason accommodate such mystical and inexplicable transmissions?

The haunted history of the U.S. Navy, that left-handed countermelody to the litany of great deeds, struggles, and sacrifice that is the Navy's evolving saga, continues to unfold, and always will. Each generation adds its layer to the supernatural side of the naval story. On October 12, 2000, a boat-borne suicide bomb blew a sixty-foot gash in the hull of the destroyer USS *Cole*, taking the lives of seventeen sailors and serving as baleful warning of ratcheting terrorism soon to culminate in the events of September 11, 2001. Reports have begun to surface of hauntings in the engineering space where the *Cole* took the hit in Yemen Harbor that terrible day. Tools move about on their own, and a witness described "a presence of someone watching you." The seventeen who perished in the blast are honored on the *Cole* in the Hall of Heroes, where a woman's voice can be heard calling out visitors' names—your name. "The ghosts," said the witness, "just want to let people know that they are watching us."

On May 22, 2008, a fire broke out on the *Nimitz*-class nuclear-powered supercarrier USS *George Washington* causing approximately $70 million in damages. It took twelve hours to extinguish the blaze, which investigators blamed on a surreptitious cigarette smoker igniting flammable liquids. All very cut-and-dried. But how interesting that the disaster occurred on this particular ship, which has been the locus of several surrealistic hauntings. What other Navy ship has ever experienced recurrent ghostly sightings of a little girl in a pink-and-white dress? Or a disappearing canine? Jingling key noises, out-of-nowhere shoulder taps, the figure of a man vanishing right through a solid bank of equipment in front of multiple witnesses— the *George Washington* had hosted an inordinate share of oddities well before the fire-story headlines appeared.

Our knowledge of such matters is as finite as the sea is vast. There are things out there benignly impervious to whether we believe in them or not, uncaring whether we can explain them away or not. They are like the squadron of ghost warships that an entire twenty-five-man crew witnessed in the mid-Atlantic in 1963. "We didn't just see them," one observer recalled, "we sailed right through their formation. We ended up right in the middle of them all. There were ships all around us. . . . Real close, too. But all of a sudden they were gone—disappeared."

Disappeared? Or did the momentary ability to see them merely expire? The ghost fleet—not just this ethereal mid-Atlantic convoy, but all the spectral ships, from all times and on all seas—is like the moon and stars in daytime; even when we cannot see them, they are still there.

And when they do come clearly into view, the ghosts of the Navy inspire complex reactions: awe, fear, perhaps even terror. But they deserve a couple of other emotions out of us as well. Pity. And above all, gratitude.

And they deserve a prayer to that power "whose arm hath bound the restless wave."

A prayer for those in peril on the sea, and locked in their wave-tossed moment for eternity.

Source Notes

The Dictionary of American Naval Fighting Ships (hereafter abbreviated as *DANFS*), a longtime Government Printing Office staple, remains the valuable first stop for basic information about ships of the U.S. Navy. It is accessible online (and searchable alphabetically) at http://www.history.navy.mil/danfs/.

Translucent Sails on Lonely Seas

The USS *Langley*'s run-in with the *Flying Dutchman* is recounted in Clary, *Superstitions of the Sea*, 133–34. For the pair of ghost ship sightings by the USS *Kennison*, see Brisbane, "U.S. Navy Meets a Phantom Ship," 41–44; see also "Vessel Sightings Defy Logical Explanation," *Augusta* (Ga.) *Chronicle*, April 4, 1999.

For accounts of the *Dash*, or "the Dead Ship of Harpswell," see Beck, *Folklore and the Sea*, 470; Norman and Scott, *Historic Haunted America*, 195–99, 202–3; Paper, "Portland's Famous Ghost Stories," 13–15; Shay, *A Sailor's Treasury*, 247–48; Simpson, *The Maine Islands in Story and Legend*, 101–3; Skinner, *Myths and Legends of Our Own Land*, 1:190–91; and Verde, *Maine Ghosts & Legends*, 7–9. The Roscoe Moulton quote is from Norman and Scott, 198–99. The quote about her speed and success is from Rowe, *The Maritime History of Maine*, 90. The quote about the ghost ship's speed "no matter which way the wind was blowing" is from Simpson, *The Maine Islands*, 102. The quote "Be it calm or storm" is from Skinner, *Myths and Legends*, 191. See also "Superstition of the Sea: 'Dead Ships' Still Believed in by Old Salts of Maine Coast," *Washington Post*, December 2, 1906.

For details of the *Dash*'s career as a privateer, see Plummer, "The Privateer 'Dash'"; and Maule and Thomas, "The Story of *Dash*."

Manifestations of Captain Jones

Callo, *John Paul Jones*; and Thomas, *John Paul Jones*, offer the two most recent biographies of Jones; Morison's classic, *John Paul Jones: A Sailor's Biography*, still retains its grandeur. See also Alden and Earle, *Makers of Naval Tradition*, 7–36; Bradford, "John Paul Jones: Honor and Professionalism," in *Command under Sail*, 18–41; and Schuon, *U.S. Navy Biographical Dictionary*, 129–31.

Stewart, *John Paul Jones: Commemoration at Annapolis*, 45–114, tells the story behind the recovery of Jones' body and explains and illustrates the corpse-and-sculpture overlay on p. 48 and in the three subsequent photographs. For more about the storage of Jones' corpse until funding for his crypt was authorized and the work completed, see Okonowicz, *Annapolis Ghosts*, 83–84.

Information about Jones haunting the John Paul Jones House in Portsmouth, New Hampshire, is from local historian and folklorist Pamela Keene's interview with the author; and from the Portsmouth Public Library's 1998 *Historic Haunted Hike* guide, 9. The female ghost living next door to (and occasionally visiting?) the John Paul Jones House was immortalized in "The White Lady of Rockingham," in Buffler, *Grandmother's Quilt*, 123–24. A consummate summation of Jones' New Hampshire sojourns is at www. seacoastnh.com.

For sightings of Jones' ghost in and around his crypt, see Annapolis ghost authority Mike Carter's report, "The Ghosts of the Naval Academy," *Annapolis Capital*, October 16, 2007; see also http://homeport.usnaweb.org/scuttlebutt. html.

Spirits in the Timbers

Toll, *Six Frigates*, 3–143, gives a definitive recent account of the founding of the Navy; the construction and launching of the *Constellation* are described on pp. 81–83. Thomas Truxtun's *Constellation* career is chronicled in Ferguson, *Truxtun of the* Constellation, 122–202.

On both the frigate and the sloop-of-war incarnations of the ship, see *DANFS, Constellation* entries. For a *Constellation* overview that encompasses both operational history and the relocation and restoration in Baltimore, see Sternlicht and Jameson, *U.S.F.* Constellation: *"Yankee Racehorse."* For *Constellation* Quasi-War battle reports, see Knox, *Naval Documents Related to the Quasi-War between the United States and France*, 2:326–45, 5:158–77; The report of the death of Neal Harvey, "killed for cowardice," is at 2:335. Many modern accounts have luridly embellished the details of Harvey's demise, describing him as being strapped to the mouth of a cannon and blown to bits. In actuality, cold sword-steel killed Harvey. Sterrett's remorseless description of Harvey's execution is also in Knox, 2:335.

The quote delineating the *Constellation* Museum's stance regarding the *"Constellation* Controversy" is from www.baltimoremuseum.org/newstore/main. html. The quote about the philosophical concept of identity continuity is in Craig, *The Shorter Routledge Encyclopedia of Philosophy*, 782.

The 1862–63 hauntings were logged in a contemporaneous diary and are available in Bopp and Bockmiller, *Showing the Flag: The Civil War Naval Diary of Moses Safford*, 22–23 (March 16, 1862, entry for death leading to hauntings), and 125–26 (June 21, 1863, entry for hauntings). For references to the 1870s ghost saluting and the 1926 fire mystery, see "Ghosts on Constellation?" in the *Baltimore News-American*, December 17, 1972.

Brougham's capturing of the ghostly quarterdeck photograph has been recounted repeatedly over the years. For the original reportage on the incident, see "'Ghost' Appears, but Navy Doesn't Give Up the Ship," *Baltimore Sun*, December 31, 1955. In a newspaper interview seventeen years later, Brougham's son accused his by-then-deceased father of having been part of a fabrication conspiracy. But the son, who now owned the photograph, refused to allow further viewing of it; see *Baltimore News-American*, December 17, 1972.

On the groundbreaking psychic investigation of the *Constellation*, see Holzer, *Window to the Past*, 153–72; and Holzer, *Ghosts*, 158–65. The groundswell of paranormal curiosity about the ship that followed the Holzer-Leek report is illustrated by "Nautical Spirits Sought on Board *Constellation*," *Baltimore Evening Sun*, November 12, 1970; and "Ghost Hunters Refused Permission to Spend Night on Frigate," *Baltimore Evening Sun*, November 26, 1970.

For the Truxtun descendants' encounter, see Randolph, "The Spirit of Commodore Truxtun," 133. For various other accounts of *Constellation* hauntings through the years, see Conboy and Conboy, "Baltimore's Spookiest Ghost Stories," 76; "Marylanders Compile Rich Legacy of Ghostly Tales and Legendary Lore," *Baltimore Sun*, October 31, 1972; and Hauck, *Haunted Places*, 206–7.

The Flaming Ghost Ship of Mahone Bay

The quote about the U.S. Navy's relationship with American privateers during the War of 1812 is from Maclay, *A History of American Privateers*, vii; for details of the rise and quick demise of the *Young Teazer*, see pp. 446–48. W. B. Dobson as an "ideal privateersman" is on p. 446. Further accounts of the *Young Teazer* can be found in Coggeshall, *History of the American Privateers, and Letters-of-Marque*, 125; Collins, *Guidebook to the Historic Sites of the War of 1812*, 337–38; Dill, *Myth, Fact, and Navigators' Secrets*, 131–33; Goold, *Portland in the Past*, 475–78; Kimball, *American Naval Battles*, 233; Murdoch, *A History of Nova Scotia*, 3:334, 360–61; and Nichols, "Notes on Nova Scotian Privateers," 135.

The quote about Johnson being a "desperate wretch . . . possessed of the devil" is from Maclay, *A History of American Privateers*, 448. The gory aftermath of the disaster and how the local population dealt with it are explained in DesBrisay, *History of the County of Lunenberg*, 518–21, which also describes the early ghost ship sightings. For the "Teazer Light" as a weather harbinger, see Beck, *Folklore and the Sea*, 101, 397. For various accounts of sightings, see Bird, *This Is Nova Scotia*, 180–89; O'Connor, *The Secret Treasure of Oak Island*, 168; and http//forum. oakislandtreasure.co.uk.

Twin Phantoms of the Mysterious Lake

Cochrane's is the seminal work regarding the Marysburgh Vortex; see *Gateway to Oblivion*, 50–53, for the area's legacy of strangeness predating the War of 1812 period. For Cochrane's speculation about the regional anomalies' influence on how war was waged, see p. 51; his *Hamilton* and *Scourge* account is on pp. 51–52.

Physical specifications and operational histories of the *Hamilton* and *Scourge* are from *DANFS*, *Hamilton* and *Scourge* entries. Lake Ontario's role in the war and the actions that unfolded there are summarized in Heidler and Heidler, *Encyclopedia of the War of 1812*, 90–91, 281–82, 293–94, 395–96, and 459–62. See also Symonds, *The Naval Institute Historical Atlas of the U.S. Navy*, 48; and Sweetman, *American Naval History*, 25–31. Myers' quotes about the storm and the sinking are culled from Cooper, *Ned Myers; or, A Life before the Mast*, chapters 5 and 6.

The quotes from the exciting firsthand account of the discovery of the twin shipwrecks are from Nelson, "*Hamilton* & *Scourge:* Ghost Ships of the War of 1812," 307–8. The quote about the *Scourge* wreck looking like she "was still prepared to sail into action against the British fleet" is from Konstam, *The History of Shipwrecks*, 159. The city of Hamilton, Ontario, provides a treasure trove of information on the *Hamilton* and *Scourge* shipwrecks at www.hamilton-scourge. hamilton.ca. On how technical advances in underwater archaeology are leading to more thorough investigations of the wrecks, see "Robotic Cameras Will Probe U.S. Ships from War of 1812," *Edmonton Journal*, May 9, 2008.

For more on the evolving efforts to research, preserve, and protect the wrecks, see "A Deep Respect for History" [the source of the Tim LeGate quote], *Ontario National Post*, March 1, 2000; "Sunken Schooners at Risk in Fight over 1812 Relics" [the source of the "at the mercy of looters" quote], *Toronto Globe and Mail*, March 5, 2005; "Canada Protects Three Shipwrecks from Scuba Diving Grave Robbers" [the source of the "scuba-diving thieves" quote], Canadian News Network, January 31, 2006.

The twin phantoms are part of a maritime region teeming with supernatural lore and unexplained oddities. For some ghostly sighting accounts, see Clary, *Superstitions of the Sea*, 134; and Stonehouse, *Haunted Lakes*, 76–78.

A Hero Remains Forever

Within a few short years Decatur went from being in need of a good modern biography to having two of them; both De Kay, *A Rage for Glory: The Life of Commodore Stephen Decatur, USN*; and Tucker, *Stephen Decatur: A Life Most Bold and Daring*, are worthy accounts of a naval hero's eventful career; see also Alden and Earle, *Makers of Naval Tradition*, 37–64; Bradford, *Command under Sail*, Decatur entry; and Schuon, *U.S. Navy Biographical Dictionary*, 56–57.

The Decatur House provides a wealth of background material on the house and its celebrated original occupant at www.decaturhouse.org; the site includes excerpts from the Decatur-Barron correspondence, which is quoted herein.

For more on the duel and Decatur's ghost, see Alexander, *Ghosts! Washington Revisited*, 26–29. For the haunting of Decatur House, see Hauck, *Haunted Places*, 111; and "Of Note: Decatur House," *Washington Post*, May 15, 1980. For the ghosts of the Bladensburg Dueling Grounds, see Hauck, *Haunted Places*, 207. Quotes about weird goings-on in general and the Decatur ghost sighting in particular are from Decatur House staff, interviews with the author.

A Fatal, Perfidious Brig

For overviews of the infamous *Somers* affair (and interpretations that diverge radically at times), see Baldwin, *Sea Fights and Shipwecks*, 184–209; Beach, *The United States Navy: 200 Years*, 177–95; Feuer, "A Question of Mutiny"; Guttridge, *Mutiny: A History of Naval Insurrection*, 87–116; Hayford, *The* Somers *Mutiny Affair*; Hunt, "The Attempted Mutiny on the U.S. Brig 'Somers'"; McFarland, *Sea Dangers: The Affair of the* Somers; Melton, *A Hanging Offense*; and Van de Water, *The Captain Called It Mutiny*.

Spencer's quote when arrested in Rio is from Rogers, "Some Reminiscences of Philip Spencer and the Brig 'Somers,'" 29. Quotes from those involved in the *Somers* executions are as presented in Mackenzie's official report and the subsequent court of inquiry; see Hayford, *The* Somers *Mutiny Affair*, 33–44, 45–48.

"The Somers: A Ballad," by Horser Clenling, appeared in the *New York Herald*, May 11, 1843; see also Hayford, *The* Somers *Mutiny Affair*, 164–68. For occult numerological and sailors' superstition aspects, see Shay, *A Sailor's Treasury*, 289–91; and Van de Water, *The Captain Called It Mutiny*, 33. For more on the *Somers* as a haunted ship, see Belcher documentary film, *The Curse of the* Somers; Rogers, "Some Reminiscences of Philip Spencer and the Brig 'Somers,'" 34–36; see also Hayford, *The* Somers *Mutiny Affair*, 210; Melton, *A Hanging Offense*, 256; and Van de Water, *The Captain Called It Mutiny*, 221.

For more on the *Somers* wreck discovery, see Delgado, "Rediscovering the *Somers*"; and Belcher, *The Curse of the* Somers. Quotes of ghostly incidents occurring during the dives are from the Belcher documentary.

The Annapolis Anomaly

For the quotes by Rosa Sutton and the ghost of Jimmie Sutton, see "Weird Claims of Spirit Testimony in Naval Tragedy," *New York Times*, November 12, 1911. The *Times* quote about the undeniable and inexplicable supernatural elements of the Sutton case is there as well.

For biographical background on Rosa Sutton, see Cutler, *A Soul on Trial*, 11–14. For anecdotes of her psychic abilities through the years, see the *New York*

Times, November 12, 1911. For information on the Marine barracks and the discovery of Sutton's body, see Cutler, *A Soul on Trial*, 1–3. For initial reaction to the case, see the *New York Times*, *Washington Post*, and *Baltimore Sun*, October 14–16, 1907.

The investigation by the American Society for Psychical Research is described in the *New York Times*, November 12, 1911, which also includes the quotes from Thacher's report. The remarks by Mary Ann Winkowski, a modern-day communicator with ghosts, are in Winkowski, *When Ghosts Speak*, 60, 81, 122.

The Sutton court of inquiry is chronicled in detail in Cutler, *A Soul on Trial*, 99–245. For Dr. Schaefer's forensic testimony, see pp. 212–14. Schaefer's "contortionist" quote about the bullet angle is on p. 214. The quote of the court's official conclusion is on p. 244. For an account of Sutton's autopsy and reburial, see pp. 259–74. The newspaper headlines are on p. 271.

Cutler's *A Soul on Trial* is the most definitive study on the Sutton case to date. The author is a Sutton family descendant, and her work is essential reading for anyone interested in this enduring mystery. For a concise yet worthwhile overview of events, see Edwards, *Strange World*, 138–41; see also Hauck, *Haunted Places*, 205. For recent Sutton ghost sightings, see Mike Carter, "The Ghosts of the Naval Academy," *Annapolis Capital*, October 16, 2007.

For other Naval Academy ghosts, see "Spooky Antics at the Naval Academy in Annapolis" [the source of the "scariest place I have ever been" quote], a testimonial posted at www.marylandghosts.com.

Haunted Bases and Other Places

Background information on Thomas Tingey and the Washington Navy Yard is available at www.history.navy.mil/bios/tingey.htm. The quote about Tingey being "the last . . . to leave the city and the first to come back" during the burning of Washington is from Commodore Thomas Tingey entry, R57/1, at www.congressionalcemetery.org. For some ghostly specifics, see Alexander, *Ghosts! Washington Revisited*; Allendorfer, "Round-shot to Rockets," 1160; "Ghosts and Rogues in Naval Gun Factory," *Washington Post*, March 19, 1958; and Hauck, *Haunted Places*, 116.

For background information on the Great Lakes Naval Training Center, see globalsecurity.org. On the supernatural side of things, see Bielski, *Chicago Haunts*, 223–26; www.castleofspirits.com; and www.theshadowlands.net. The U.S. Naval Postgraduate School's lingering ghosts are described in Hauck, *Haunted Places*, 58; and at www.hauntedhouses.com.

The fiery disaster at the Tracy House is in "General Tracy Stricken: Wife and Daughter Both Die a Terrible Death," *New York Times*, February 4, 1890; and "The Washington Tragedy," *New York Times*, February 5, 1890. Alexander, *Ghosts! Washington Revisited*, 82–83, gives a thorough account of the death house's ghostly history before the Tracys took up residence there; see also Hauck, *Haunted Places*, 112.

For the sad southern ghost that hovers at Charleston Naval Base, see Hauck, *Haunted Places*, 375; Leiding, *Historic Houses of South Carolina*, 12–13; and Martin, *Charleston Ghosts*, 5–10. The ghosts of a colonial carriage mishap that still haunt Yorktown's U.S. Naval Weapons Station are depicted in Hauck, *Haunted Places*, 442. Hauck delineates the numerous specters populating the U.S. Naval Shipyard at Norfolk on p. 433; Naval Air Station Norfolk's mess hall phantom and the mysterious nude apparition of Dam Neck Naval Base are described at www.theshadowlands.net.

The naval officer ghost at Lynch Hall is also described at www.theshadowlands.net, as well as being mentioned in the University of Pittsburgh at Greensburg's *University Times* 36, no. 7, November 20, 2003; and at www.pitt.edu/~upg/LynchHall.html. The main account of Admiral Hawley's ghost and the haunting of Mizzentop is in Holzer, *Yankee Ghosts*, 158–71. One of the principal witnesses erroneously stated that Admiral Hawley died in 1933, a mistake perpetuated in some subsequent accounts; he actually died in 1925; see obituary, "Rear Admiral Hawley Dies at 79 Years," *New York Times*, February 11, 1925.

For a biographical survey of David Glasgow Farragut, see William N. Still Jr., "David Glasgow Farragut: The Union's Nelson," in Bradford, *Captains of the Old Steam Navy*, 166–89. See also Alden and Earle, *Makers of Naval Tradition*, 146–75; and Schuon, *U.S. Navy Biographical Dictionary*, 73–74. For accounts of Farragut's ghost, see "Civil War Hero Haunts Quarters 'A' at Navy Yard," *Portsmouth* (N.H.) *Herald*, May 19, 2002; and "Legacy of Life in Shipyard's Quarters A," *Portsmouth* (N.H.) *Herald*, July 27, 2003.

Battleships of the Dead

The physical specifications and operational history of the *Texas* are detailed in *DANFS*, *Texas* (BB–35) entry; and Paine, *Ships of the World*, 512–13. The *Texas* ghost is investigated in Williams, *Haunted Texas*, 6–7; at www.lonestarspirits.org; and at www.theshadowlands.net.

The physical specifications and operational history of the *North Carolina* are detailed in *DANFS*, *North Carolina* (BB–55) entry; and Paine, *Ships of the World*, 366. Bradshaw's memoir, *Ghosts on the Battleship* North Carolina, is an invaluable resource for the warship paranormalist; Bradshaw quotes in this chapter are from pp. 5, 18, 23, 24, 28, 30, 40, and 42–43. The exception is Bradshaw's "I don't want to die here" quote, which is from "USS *North Carolina*'s Watchman Believes It's a Haunted Ship," *Greensboro News-Record*, October 31, 2002. See also "Legend Sparks Ghost Hunts," *Daily Tarheel*, March 3, 2004; and "Ghost Hunter Shadows Aycock Auditorium," *Greensboro News-Record*, May 27, 2006. The investigation by the Atlantic Paranormal Society can be viewed in *Ghost Hunters: Season Two*, episode: "Mordecai House and USS *North Carolina*."

Echoes of Infamy

For a summary of the unfolding events of the Pearl Harbor attack, see *DANFS*, *Arizona* (BB–39) entry; Paine, *Ships of the World*, 36; Sweetman, *American Naval History*, 145; and Symonds, *The Naval Institute Historical Atlas of the U.S. Navy*, 140.

For Pearl Harbor ghosts, see Belanger, *Encyclopedia of Haunted Places*, 216–17; Crain, *Haunted U.S. Battlefields*, 186–90 (the psychic's quotes are from p. 189); and www.hauntedamericatours.com (source of the "Top Ten Most Haunted Battlefields" designation). Dan Lenihan's poignant and reflective account of diving on the *Arizona* wreck, "*Arizona* Revisited," is posted by the USS *Arizona* Preservation Project at www.pastfoundation.org/Arizona/index.htm.

The pensive ghost of Midway is covered in "Tales of Ghost Greet *Hokule'a*," *Honolulu Advertiser*, June 20, 2004.

Blue-Eyed Charlie and Shadow Ed

A description and operational history of the USS *Lexington* are in *DANFS*, *Lexington* (CV–16) entry; and in Paine, *Ships of the World*, 302. The *Lexington* Museum's thorough Web site also serves up a cornucopia of historical data at www.usslexington.com.

The Kinnick story is recounted in Fimrite, "Nile Kinnick: With the Wartime Death of the '39 Heisman Winner, America Lost a Leader," 112–24. The reporter's quote about Kinnick's Heisman speech is on p. 116, as are Kinnick's diary entry about the beauty of flight and the friend's quote about Kinnick's "aura." Kinnick's "May God give me the courage" quote is on p. 123. The friend's quote about being shocked by Kinnick's death is from "Everybody's All-America," an online Kinnick biography at espn.go.com. On hauntings on the *Lexington*, see "About the *Lexington* Ghost," *Corpus Christi Caller-Times*, October 31, 1994; "'Charly': The 'Blue Ghost's' Ghost," www.militaryhistory.about.com; "Haunted Ships: The USS *Lexington* in Corpus Christi, Texas," www.haunted-places-to-go.com; and "The Polite Haunting of the Blue Ghost," www.wintertexansonline.com.

The characteristics and chronology of the USS *Yorktown* are recorded in *DANFS*, *Yorktown* (CV–10) entry; and in Paine, *Ships of the World*, 584. Security guard and visitor accounts of *Yorktown* ghost sightings are at www.yorktownsailor.com/yorktown/ghost.htm. The ectoplasmic photograph is described and displayed at www.angelsghosts.com/uss_yorktown_ghost_picture.html.

Brothers to the End, and Beyond

The story of the USS *The Sullivans* is the story of two ships, really. The *Juneau* is described in *DANFS*, *Juneau* entry; and in Paine, *Ships of the World*, 279. The *Sullivans* is in *DANFS*, *The Sullivans* entry; and in Paine, *Ships of the World*, 513–

14. Kurzman's searing account, *Left to Die: The Tragedy of the USS* Juneau, lays bare the tragedy; for the Sullivan brothers in particular, see pp. 10–26, 166–67, and 245–49. See also "The Sullivan Brothers: The Loss of USS *Juneau* (CL–52)," at www.history.navy.mil; "Worst Family Catastrophe in Naval History: 5 Brothers Lost Together as Their Ship Goes Down in Solomons," *Washington Post,* January 13, 1943; and "Sullivans Typify War Spirit of U.S.," *New York Times,* February 8, 1943. Alleta Sullivan's letter to President Roosevelt and Roosevelt's condolence letter are both viewable at www.archives.gov.

Accounts of hauntings aboard *The Sullivans* are given in Hauck, *Haunted Places,* 293; Revai, *Haunted New York,* 59–60; and at www.theflagship.net.

A Hornet's Nest of Hauntings

For *Hornet* background, see *DANFS, Hornet* (CV–12) entry. The headless ghost is described at www.tv.com/fear/u.s.s.-hornet/episode/137697/recap.html?tag=overview;recap. The engine room phantom is chronicled there, too; and in Gault, "Is the USS *Hornet* (CV-12) Really Haunted?" 17. The sick-bay specter, the "amoeba-like plasma" glow, the pipe-smoking ghost, and sundry other accounts are gathered at a *Hornet* ghost sighting testimonial page at http://www.its.caltech.edu/~drmiles/ghost_stories.html. For the mess hall ghost, see Gault, 24; the kamikaze ghost is recounted at the two aforementioned web pages and in Gault, 24–25, which quotes the witness who made the mistake of lying down on the wrong cot at the wrong time. The Bob Messiah quote also is from Gault, 24. The TV news reporter is quoted in Gault, 17, 24. The McKean account and quotes and the Rogers account are from Mackenzie, "*Hornet* Redefines 'Presence,'" 40; Tallmadge's testimony follows on p. 41. LaDue's description of the Christmas tree incident is on p. 39. The Loyd Auerbach quotes are from Mackenzie, 41; and Auerbach, "Psychic Frontiers: A Ship of Souls."

Of Hangars and Their Hangers-On

For the ghosts of Pensacola, see Hauck, *Haunted Places,* 125; Jenkins, *Florida's Ghostly Legends and Folklore,* 3:12–20; Manuel, *Pensacola Bay: A Military History,* 121; and www.cnic.navy.mil/Pensacola/AboutCNIC/GeneralInformation/HistoricSites/Building16/index.htm.

For the ghosts of Olathe, see Myers, *A Ghosthunter's Guide to Haunted Landmarks, Parks, Churches, and Other Public Places,* 93–100; "Things That Go Bump in the Night: New Century Air Center," *Blue Valley Northwest* 11, no. 2, October 24, 2003; www.theflagship.net; www.kansasghosts.com; www.leftfield-psi.net/ghosts/haunted_places/usa_k.html; and www.theshadowlands.net. The earliest news account of the crash that spawned the hauntings is in the *Olathe Mirror,* January 6, 1949.

For the ghosts of Miramar, see "Haunted History Spooks Hangar One," *Marine Corps News*, January 9, 2004. For coverage of the crash, see "Miramar Disaster! Jet Smashes Hangar—15 Killed," *San Diego Tribune*, December 22, 1969; "Heroism Cut Miramar Toll," *San Diego Tribune*, December 23, 1969; "Navy to Call Inquiry Board into Cause of F8 Disaster," *San Diego Tribune*, December 23, 1969; "Memorial Rites Slated Friday for Jet Crash Victims," *San Diego Union*, December 24, 1969; and "Services Honor 11 Victims of Miramar Crash," *San Diego Union*, December 27, 1969.

Hell's Flight Deck

Freeman's *Sailors to the End* is the definitive work on the *Forrestal* conflagration; for how old, inferior bombs helped exacerbate the catastrophe, see pp. 80–88; for a gripping and detailed account of the fire and the sailors' heroic response, see pp. 90–223.

On the *Forrestal* hauntings, see "*Forrestal* Ghost," Associated Press, August 6, 1988; Hauck, *Haunted Places*, 433–34; www.angelfire.com; www.theshadowlands. net; and www.urbanchillers.com.

For Those in Peril on the Sea

The World War II incident of the just-killed sailor appearing at his lover's bedside back in the United States is chronicled at www.ghost-stalker.com. A firsthand account of the ghost of the electrocuted petty officer is given at www.theshadow-lands.net, which also contains reports of the USS *Cole* hauntings and the bizarre apparitions sighted on the USS *George Washington*. The Atlantic ghost squadron sighting of 1963 is described in Bauman, "Phantoms of the Sea."

Bibliography

Alden, Carroll S., and Ralph Earle. *Makers of Naval Tradition*. Boston: Ginn and Company, 1925.

Alexander, John. *Ghosts! Washington Revisited: The Ghostlore of the Nation's Capital*. Atglen, Pa.: Schiffer, 1998.

Allendorfer, Lt. Cdr. Harry C., USN. "Round-shot to Rockets: The Story of the Washington Navy Yard and Naval Gun Factory." U.S. Naval Institute *Proceedings* 75, no. 10 (1949): 1159–65.

Auerbach, Loyd. "Psychic Frontiers: A Ship of Souls." *FATE* 52, no. 10 (1999). Available at www.mindreader.com/articles/fate1099.doc.

Baldwin, Hanson W. *Sea Fights and Shipwrecks: True Tales of the Seven Seas*. Garden City, N.Y.: Doubleday, 1938; reprint, 1955.

Bauman, Richard. "Phantoms of the Sea." *FATE* 54, no. 11 (2001). Available at http://fatemag.com/issues/2000s/2001=11article1a.html.

Beach, Capt. Edward L., USN (Ret.). *The United States Navy: 200 Years*. New York: Henry Holt, 1986.

Beck, Horace. *Folklore and the Sea*. Middletown, Conn.: Marine Historical Association, 1973.

Belanger, Jeff, ed. *Encyclopedia of Haunted Places: Ghostly Locales from around the World*. Edison, N.J.: Castle Books, 2008.

Belcher, George, director. *The Curse of the Somers: Billy Budd's Ghost Ship*. Film documentary. San Francisco: Somers Documentary Film Project Limited Partnership, 1995.

Bielski, Ursula. *Chicago Haunts: Ghostlore of the Windy City*. Chicago: Lake Claremont Press, 1998.

Bird, Will R. *This Is Nova Scotia*. Toronto: McGraw-Hill, 1972.

Bopp, Lawrence J., and Stephen R. Bockmiller, eds. *Showing the Flag: The Civil War Naval Diary of Moses Safford, USS* Constellation. Charleston, S.C.: History Press, 2004.

Bradford, James C., ed. *Captains of the Old Steam Navy: Makers of the American Naval Tradition, 1840–1880.* Annapolis: Naval Institute Press, 1986.

———. *Command under Sail: Makers of the American Naval Tradition, 1775–1850.* Annapolis: Naval Institute Press, 1985.

Bradshaw, Danny. *Ghosts on the Battleship* North Carolina. Wilmington, N.C.: Bradshaw Publishing Company, 2002.

Brisbane, Howard H. "U.S. Navy Meets a Phantom Ship." *FATE* 15, no. 4 (1962): 41–44.

Buffler, Esther. *Grandmother's Quilt.* Francestown, N.H.: Golden Quill Press, 1988.

Callo, Joseph. *John Paul Jones: America's First Sea Warrior.* Annapolis: Naval Institute Press, 2006.

Clary, James. *Superstitions of the Sea: A Digest of Beliefs, Customs, and Mystery.* St. Clair, Mich.: Maritime History in Art, 1994.

Cochrane, Hugh. *Gateway to Oblivion: The Great Lakes' Bermuda Triangle.* New York: Doubleday, 1980.

Coggeshall, George. *History of the American Privateers, and Letters-of-Marque, during Our War with England in the Years 1812, '13 and '14.* New York: George Putnam, 1861.

Collins, Gilbert. *Guidebook to the Historic Sites of the War of 1812.* 2nd ed. Toronto: Dundurn Group, 2006.

Conboy, Don, and Marian Conboy. "Baltimore's Spookiest Ghost Stories." *Baltimore* magazine (October 1979): 75–77.

Cooper, James Fenimore. *Ned Myers; or, A Life before the Mast.* New ed. Intro. William S. Dudley. Annapolis: Naval Institute Press, 1989.

Craig, Edward, ed. *The Shorter Routledge Encyclopedia of Philosophy.* London and New York: Routledge, 2005.

Crain, Mary Beth. *Haunted U.S. Battlefields: Ghosts, Hauntings, and Eerie Events from America's Fields of Honor.* Guilford, Conn.: Globe Pequot Press, 2008.

Cutler, Robin R. *A Soul on Trial: A Marine Corps Mystery at the Turn of the Twentieth Century.* Lanham, Md.: Rowman and Littlefield, 2007.

De Kay, James T. *A Rage for Glory: The Life of Commodore Stephen Decatur, USN*. New York: Free Press, 2004.

Delgado, James P. "Rediscovering the *Somers*." *Naval History* 8, no. 2 (1994): 28–31.

DesBrisay, Mather B. *History of the County of Lunenberg*. 2nd ed. Toronto: William Briggs, 1895.

Dill, J. Gregory. *Myth, Fact, and Navigators' Secrets: Incredible Tales of the Sea and Sailors*. Guilford, Conn.: Globe Pequot Press, 2006.

Edwards, Frank. *Strange World*. Secaucus, N.J.: Lyle Stuart, 1964.

Ferguson, Eugene S. *Truxtun of the* Constellation. Annapolis: Naval Institute Press, 1982.

Feuer, A. B. "A Question of Mutiny." *Naval History* 8, no. 2 (1994): 22–27.

Fimrite, Ron. "Nile Kinnick: With the Wartime Death of the '39 Heisman Winner, America Lost a Leader." *Sports Illustrated* 67, no. 9 (1987): 112–24.

Freeman, Gregory A. *Sailors to the End: The Deadly Fire on the USS* Forrestal *and the Heroes Who Fought It*. New York: William Morrow, 2002.

Gault, Owen. "Is the USS *Hornet* (CV-12) Really Haunted?" *Sea Classics* 41, no. 4 (2008): 14–17, 24–25.

Goold, William. *Portland in the Past, with Historical Notes of Old Falmouth*. Portland, Maine: B. Thurston, 1886.

Guttridge, Leonard F. *Mutiny: A History of Naval Insurrection*. Annapolis: Naval Institute Press, 1992.

Hauck, Dennis W. *Haunted Places: The National Directory*. Rev. ed. New York: Penguin Books, 2002.

Hayford, Harrison, ed. *The* Somers *Mutiny Affair: A Book of Primary Source Materials*. Englewood Cliffs, N.J.: Prentice-Hall, 1959.

Heidler, David S., and Jeanne T. Heidler, eds. *Encyclopedia of the War of 1812*. Annapolis: Naval Institute Press, 2004.

Holzer, Hans. *Ghosts: True Encounters with the World Beyond*. New York: Black Dog and Leventhal, 1997.

———. *Window to the Past: Exploring History through ESP*. Garden City, N.Y.: Doubleday, 1969.

———. *Yankee Ghosts: Spine-Tingling Encounters with the Phantoms of New York and New England*. Dublin, N.H.: Yankee Books, 1988.

Hunt, Rear Adm. Livingston, USN (Ret.). "The Attempted Mutiny on the U.S. Brig 'Somers.'" U.S. Naval Institute *Proceedings* 51, no. 273 (1925): 2062–2100.

James, William. *Naval Occurrences of the War of 1812*. London: Conway Maritime Press, 2004. Reprint of 1817 private edition.

Jenkins, Greg. *Florida's Ghostly Legends and Folklore*. Vol. 3: *The Gulf Coast and Peninsula*. Sarasota, Fla.: Pineapple Press, 2007.

Kimball, Horace, ed. *American Naval Battles: Being a Complete History of the Battles Fought by the Navy of the United States from Its Establishment in 1794 to the Present Time*. Boston: J. J. Smith Jr., 1831.

Knox, Capt. Dudley W., USN (Ret.), et al., eds. *Naval Documents Related to the Quasi-War between the United States and France*. 7 vols. Washington, D.C.: U.S. Government Printing Office, 1935.

Konstam, Angus. *The History of Shipwrecks*. New York: Lyons Press, 1999.

Kurzman, Dan. *Left to Die: The Tragedy of the USS Juneau*. New York: Simon and Schuster, 1994.

Leiding, Harriette Kershaw. *Historic Houses of South Carolina*. Philadelphia: J. B. Lippincott, 1921.

Mackenzie, Lily I. "*Hornet* Redefines 'Presence.'" *Naval History* 14, no. 6 (2000): 38–42.

Maclay, Edgar S. *A History of American Privateers*. New York: D. Appleton, 1899.

Manuel, Dale. *Pensacola Bay: A Military History*. Charleston, S.C.: Arcadia Publishing, 2004.

Martin, Margaret R. *Charleston Ghosts*. Columbia: University of South Carolina Press, 1963.

Maule, Elizabeth S., and Randall W. Thomas. "The Story of *Dash*." *DASH: The Newsletter of the Freeport Historical Society* (Summer 2004): 1–3.

McFarland, Philip. *Sea Dangers: The Affair of the* Somers. New York: Schocken Books, 1985.

Melton, Buckner F., Jr. *A Hanging Offense: The Strange Affair of the Warship* Somers. New York: Free Press, 2003.

Morison, Samuel E. *John Paul Jones: A Sailor's Biography*. Boston: Little, Brown, 1959.

Murdoch, Beamish, Esq., Q.C. *A History of Nova Scotia, or Acadie*. Halifax, Nova Scotia: James Barnes, 1867.

Myers, Arthur. *A Ghosthunter's Guide to Haunted Landmarks, Parks, Churches, and Other Public Places.* Chicago: Contemporary Books, 1993.

Nelson, Daniel A. *"Hamilton* & *Scourge:* Ghost Ships of the War of 1812." *National Geographic* (March 1983): 289–313.

Nichols, George E. E. "Notes on Nova Scotian Privateers." *Collections of the Royal Nova Scotia Historical Society* 13 (1903): 111–52.

Norman, Michael, and Beth Scott. *Historic Haunted America.* New York: Tor, 1995.

O'Connor, D'Arcy. *The Secret Treasure of Oak Island: The Amazing Story of a Centuries-Old Treasure Hunt.* Guilford, Conn.: Globe Pequot Press, 2004.

Okonowicz, Ed. *Annapolis Ghosts: History, Mystery, Legends and Lore.* Elkton, Md.: Myst and Lace, 2007.

Paine, Lincoln P. *Ships of the World: An Historical Encyclopedia.* Boston: Houghton Mifflin, 1997.

Paper, Henry. "Portland's Famous Ghost Stories." *Greater Portland* 30, no. 5 (1985): 10–20.

Plummer, E. C. "The Privateer 'Dash.'" *New England* magazine 16, no. 5 (1894): 568–71.

Randolph, Evan. "The Spirit of Commodore Truxtun: A Family Reunion, a Famous Ship, and a Ghost." *Yankee* (June 1977): 80–85, 132–37.

Revai, Cheri. *Haunted New York: Ghosts and Strange Phenomena of the Empire State.* Mechanicsburg, Pa.: Stackpole Books, 2005.

Rogers, Robert C. [writing as R.C.R.]. "Some Reminiscences of Philip Spencer and the Brig 'Somers.'" *The United Service: A Monthly Review of Military and Naval Affairs,* n.s., 4 (July 1890): 23–36.

Rowe, William Hutchinson. *The Maritime History of Maine: Three Centuries of Shipbuilding and Seafaring.* New York: W. W. Norton, 1948.

Schuon, Karl. *U.S. Navy Biographical Dictionary.* New York: Franklin Watts, 1964.

Shay, Frank. *A Sailor's Treasury.* New York: W. W. Norton, 1951.

Simpson, Dorothy. *The Maine Islands in Story and Legend.* 9 vols. Philadelphia: J. B. Lippincott, 1960.

Skinner, Charles M. *Myths and Legends of Our Own Land.* Philadelphia: J. B. Lippincott, 1896.

Sternlicht, Sanford, and Edwin M. Jameson. *U.S.F. Constellation: "Yankee Racehorse."* Cockeysville, Md.: Liberty Publishing, 1981.

Stewart, Charles W., ed. *John Paul Jones: Commemoration at Annapolis, April 24, 1906.* Washington, D.C.: Government Printing Office, 1907.

Stonehouse, Frederick. *Haunted Lakes: Great Lakes Ghost Stories, Superstitions and Sea Serpents.* Duluth, Minn.: Lake Superior Port Cities Inc., 1997.

Sweetman, Jack. *American Naval History: An Illustrated Chronology of the U.S. Navy and Marine Corps, 1775–Present.* 3rd ed. Annapolis: Naval Institute Press, 2002.

Symonds, Craig L. *The Naval Institute Historical Atlas of the U.S. Navy.* Annapolis: Naval Institute Press, 1995.

Thomas, Evan. *John Paul Jones: Sailor, Hero, Father of the American Navy.* New York: Simon and Schuster, 2003.

Toll, Ian. *Six Frigates: The Epic History of the Founding of the U.S. Navy.* New York: W. W. Norton, 2006.

Tucker, Spencer. *Stephen Decatur: A Life Most Bold and Daring.* Annapolis: Naval Institute Press, 2005.

Van de Water, Frederick F. *The Captain Called It Mutiny.* New York: Ives Washburn, 1954.

Verde, Thomas A. *Maine Ghosts & Legends: 26 Encounters with the Supernatural.* Camden, Maine: Down East Books, 1989.

Williams, Scott. *Haunted Texas: A Travel Guide.* Guilford, Conn.: Globe Pequot Press, 2007.

Winkowski, Mary Ann. *When Ghosts Speak: Understanding the World of Earthbound Spirits.* New York: Grand Central Publishing, 2007.

Index

Adams, John Quincy, 45, 51
air stations: Miramar Naval Air
  Station, 135–37; Olathe Naval Air
  Station, 134–35; Pensacola Naval
  Air Station, 132–34
Alameda, California, 123
Alexander, 31
Algiers, 49
America, 13
American Revolution, 13–14, 17, 83,
  107, 123
American Society for Psychical
  Research, 74
Ann (Great Britain), 31
Apollo 8 mission, 114
Apollo 11 mission, 124
Arizona: attack on, 100–101, 104, 117;
  christening of, 103; dives to examine
  and map, 102–3; ghosts of, 101,
  102–4
Arizona Preservation Project, 102–3
Arkansas, 90
Armistice, 5
Atlantic Paranormal Society (TAPS),
  99
Auerbach, Loyd, 128, 130

Balboa, Daniel, 140
Ball, Bill, 117
Ballard, Robert, 43
Barbary wars, 17, 18, 20, 46, 49
Barron, James, 48–49, 50–52
bear, 39
Beirut, 121

Belcher, George, 68–69
Belcher, Joel, 69
Bethesda Naval Hospital, 138
Betty Macomber, 7–8
Bibber, Simon, 7
Bladensburg Dueling Grounds, 51–52,
  53
Blue Ghost, 106. See also Lexington
Board of Navy Commissioners, 50
Boleyn, Anne, 11
Bon Homme Richard (Duc de Duras),
  13
Bradshaw, Danny, 95–98
Brant, Rosa, 70
Brougham, Allan Ross, 22–23
Buffalo, New York, 121
Buffer, Esther, 14
Burleigh, David, 136

California, 101
Campbell, John, 21
Caroline Islands, 120
Carvel Hall, 72
Casco Bay, Maine, 2–3, 5–7
Castor (Great Britain), 32
Cayuga, 44
Champlain, 6
Charleston Naval Base, 82
"Charlie," 107, 110–12, 113
Chauncey, Isaac, 36, 39–40
Cherbourg, Battle of, 91, 93
Chesapeake, 48
Civil War, 77, 86–87, 132–33
Cochrane, Hugh, 36, 41

Cold War, 121
Cole, 143
Collins, Mort, 7
Constellation: building and launching of, 17–18; crew of, 47; fire aboard, 21; France, fight with, 18–20; frigate configuration, 18–20; ghosts of, 21–28, 93; museum of, 21; nickname of, 20; rebuilding of, 20–21; sloop-of-war configuration, 20–21, 27; World War II role, 22
Constitution, 22
Continental Navy, 17
Coolidge, Calvin, 90
Cooper, James Fenimore, 37
Coral Sea, Battle of the, 104, 107
Corpus Christi, Texas, 106
Corry Field, 134
Cousteau, Jacques, 43
Crocker, Charles, 81
Cromwell, Samuel, 62–64
Crooks, James, 37
Crowninshield, Benjamin, 50
Cuban Missile Crisis, 109, 121

Dam Neck Naval Base, Virginia Beach, 83–84
Daniels, Josephus, 103
Dash: career of, 4–7; design of, 4; ghost of, 3, 7–9
"The Dead Ship of Harpswell" (Whittier), 8, 9
Deal, David, 110
Decatur, James, 47
Decatur, Stephen, Jr.: avenging brother's death, 47–48; Barron court-martial, 48–49; Barron duel, 50–52; career of, 48, 49–50; character of, 45–46; death of, 52; duel fighting, 46; early life of, 45; Enterprise, 46; ghost of, 45, 52–54; heroism of, 45, 49; Philadelphia, 46
Decatur, Stephen, Sr., 45
Decatur, Susan Wheeler, 48, 50, 51, 52

Decatur House, 45, 50, 52–54
Del Monte Hotel, 81
Diana, 36. See also Hamilton
Digges, Edward, 82
Dobson, W. B., 30, 31–32
Dolphin, 56
Doolittle raid, 124
Dreadnought (Great Britain), 89, 138
dreadnoughts, 89. See also Texas
Duc de Duras (Bon Homme Richard), 13

Eastern Solomons, Battle of, 94
Edmund Fitzgerald, 44
electromagnetic phenomena, 35–36, 94
Elliott, Jesse, 50–51
Enterprise, 46, 137
Erie, Lake, 38
Essex-class carriers, 107, 110, 113, 123

Fairfield, 56
Farragut, David Glasgow, 86–88, 89
Fighting Lady, 113. See also Yorktown
"Firestal," 140. See also Forrestal
Flannelly, Joseph, 120
fleet of the dead, 1, 29, 142–44
Fletcher-class destroyer, 120
Flintlock, Operation, 113
Flying Dutchman, 1–2, 33
Ford Island Airfield, 101, 102
"Forrest Fire," 140. See also Forrestal
Forrestal: career of, 138–40; decommissioning, 141; fire aboard, 139–40, 141; ghosts of, 140–41; launching of, 138; naming of, 138; nickname of, 140; systems on, 138; Vietnam War, 138–39, 141
Forrestal, James V., 138
Fort George, 38, 39
France: America as gift to, 13; Constellation's fight with, 18–20; Duc de Duras (Bon Homme Richard), 13
Franklin, Benjamin, 13
Fuqua, Samuel G., 101

Gansevoort, Guert, 61
geographically dispersed hauntings,
    11–12, 14–16
"George," 140
George Washington, 143
German U-boats, 3
ghost aircraft, 132
ghost fleet, 1, 29, 142–44
Ghost Hunters, 99
Gilbert Islands, 113
Gonsalves, Steve, 99
Great Lakes Naval Training Center,
    Chicago, 79–81, 117
Guadalcanal, 95, 118–19
Guam, 113, 116, 123

Hall, Guy B., 133–34
Halligan Hall, 71–72
Hamilton: ghost of, 35, 44; renaming
    of, 36–37; shipwreck, 36, 42–44;
    sinking of ships with same name, 42;
    storm and sinking of, 41–42; War of
    1812, 35, 37–38, 40, 41
Hamilton, Ontario, 43–44
Hamilton, Paul, 37
Hansen, Carl, 25, 26
Harrison, Benjamin, 81
Harvey, Neal, 20, 26, 28
Haunted North Carolina, 99
Hawes, Jason, 99
Hawley, J. H., 85–86
Henderson Field, 118
Hickam Airfield/Hickam Air Force
    Base, 101, 102
Hillard, James, 141
La Hogue (Great Britain), 31–32
Holzer, Hans, 25–26, 85–86
Hornet: decommissioning, 124,
    129–30; ghost aircraft, 132; ghosts
    of, 123, 124–31; high-risk working
    environment, 123, 124–25; kamikaze
    attack attempt, 126; launch and
    christening of, 123; museum status,
    123, 128–30; naming of, 123; post-

World War II career, 124; sinking
    of ships with same name, 123, 132;
    sister ships, 124; World War II duty,
    123–24
Hornet Foundation, 128–29
Hotel Del Monte, 81
Houdon, Jean-Antoine, 14

Independence, 56
L'Insurgente (France), 19, 47
Invincible Napoleon (France), 30–31
ironclad monitors, 89
Iwo Jima, 91–92, 124

Jackson, Andrew, 6
James, Reuben, 47
"John Paul," 83
John Paul Jones House Museum,
    14–15
Johnson, Frederick, 30, 32, 33
Johnson County Industrial Airport,
    134
Jones, John Paul, 11–16; crypt, 14,
    15–16, 77; as father of U.S. Navy,
    13–14, 17; geographically dispersed
    hauntings, 11–12, 14–16, 77; life of,
    12–14
Juneau, 118–19, 121

Kennison, 2
Kidd, Isaac C., 100
Kingston, Ontario, 37–38
Kinnick, Nile Clark, Jr., 107–9, 111
Knight, William, 136–37
Korean War, 121
Kwajalein, 109, 120

La Hogue (Great Britain), 31–32
La Vengeance (France), 20, 47
Lacedemonian (Great Britain), 5
LaDue, Keith, 129, 130
Langdon, Mrs. Woodbury, 14–15
Langdon, Woodbury, 14
Langley, 1–2

Laotian Crisis, 109
Last of the Dreadnoughts, 89. See also Texas
Latrobe, Benjamin Henry, 50, 78
Leecock, Richard, 65
Leek, Sybil, 25–26, 85–86
Legate, Tim, 43
Lenihan, Dan, 102–4
Leopard (Great Britain), 48
Lexington: building and launching of, 107; decommissioning, 110; ghosts of, 106–7, 110–12, 113; museum status, 106, 110–12; naming of, 107; nickname of, 106; post-World War II career, 109–10; ships with same name, 107; sinking of, premature declarations of, 106; sister ships, 113, 123; women aboard, 110; World War II role, 107–9, 113
Leyte Gulf, Battle of, 109, 124
Lincoln, Abraham, 11, 87
L'Insurgente (France), 19, 47
Lone Star Spirits, 93–94
Lord Nelson (Canada), 37. See also Scourge
Luzon, 109
Lynch, Charles McKenna, 84–85
Lynch Hall, University of Pittsburgh, 84–85

MacArthur, Douglas, 113
Macedonian (Great Britain), 49
Mackenzie, Alexander Slidell: career of, 56–57; character of, 58; death of, 65; defense of executions, 65; discipline aboard Somers, 59–60; discipline methods, 56, 57; judgement about executions, 65; literary career, 56–57; mutinous plan and executions to punish, 61–65; reputation of, 56–57; Somers command, 56, 57; Somers voyage to Africa, 59–65
Madison, James, 48

Magic Carpet, Operation, 92
magnetic anomalies, 35–36, 42, 94, 130
Mahan Hall, 75
Mahone Bay, Nova Scotia, 32–34
Manly (Great Britain), 32
Mariana Islands, 109, 113, 120, 124
Marine Corps Air Station Miramar, 137
Marshall Islands, 113
Maryland, 101
Marysburgh Vortex, 35–36
Matheson, Chip, 69
Matsu island, 114
McCain, John, 139
McKean, Alan, 128–29
McNair, Matthew, 36
Messiah, Bob, 127
Mexican War, 66–68
Midway, Battle of, 104, 113, 116, 123, 132
Midway Atoll, 104–5
"Might FID," 140. See also Forrestal
Miramar Naval Air Station, 135–37
Missouri, 57
Mizzentop, 85–86
Mobile Bay, Battle of, 87, 89
Moulton, Roscoe, 7
Murray, Stache Margaret, 128
Myers, Ned, 37, 38–41

National Geographic Society, 43
National Park Service, Submerged Resource Center, 102–3
Native (Great Britain), 31
Naval School, 71. See also U.S. Naval Academy
Navy-Marine Corps Trial Judiciary, Trial Service Office, 134
Nelson, Daniel, 42–43
Nevada, 101
New Century Air Center, 134
New Orleans, Battle of, 6, 87, 89
New York-class battleships, 89
Nimitz-class nuclear-powered supercarrier, 143

Norfolk Naval Air Station, 83
North Carolina: building and
    launching of, 94; ghosts of, 94, 95–
    99; museum status, 95–99; nickname
    of, 94; World War II role, 94–95

Office of Paranormal Investigations
    (OPI), 128
Okinawa, 92, 95, 114, 120, 124, 142
Oklahoma, 101
Olathe Naval Air Station, 134–35
Oneida, 37
Ontario, Lake: Cayuga, 44; Hamilton,
    35, 36–38, 40, 41–44; Marysburgh
    Vortex, 35–36; phenomena on,
    41; Scourge, 35, 36, 37–42, 43–44;
    shipbuilding on, 37–38; Sophiasburg
    Triangle, 36
Ontario Heritage Act, 44
Oriskany, 136
Ormoc Bay, 124
Orpheus (Great Britain), 32

Pactolus (Great Britain), 5
Palau Islands, 120
Patriot's Point, Charleston, 113, 115
Pearl Harbor: attack on, 100–101, 104;
    dramatization of, 114; ghosts of,
    101–4
Pennock, A. M., 87
Pennsylvania-class battleships, 100
Pensacola Lighthouse, 133
Pensacola Naval Air Station, 132–34
Pensacola Naval Hospital, 132–33
Perry, Matthew Calbraith, 57
Perry, Oliver Hazard, 38
Philadelphia, 46, 47, 48
Philippine Sea, Battle of the, 109, 113,
    123
Pike, 22
Port Moresby, New Guinea, 118
Porter, John, 5–6
Porter, Lois, 6–7
Porter, Seward, 4

Portsmouth Naval Shipyard, 87–88
Potomac, 59
Preble, Edward, 46
President, 49
privateers, 4–5, 6, 10, 29
Profitt, Al, 98–99

Quantico, 71
Quemoy island, 114

Ranger, 13
Rattlesnake, 32
"Red," 90, 93–94
Revolutionary War, 13–14, 17, 83, 107,
    123
Rockingham Hotel, 14–15
Rogers, Bob, 129
Rogers, John, 19–20
Rogers, Robert C., 66–68
Roosevelt, Franklin, 22, 120
Roosevelt, Theodore, 14, 79
Rota, 123
Royal Ontarion Museum, 43
Ruse, Thomas, 135

Sacket's Harbor, New York, 37–38
Saipan, 113, 123
San Diego, California, 135. See also
    Miramar Naval Air Station
San Domingo (Great Britain), 30
Santa Cruz Islands, Battle of, 123
Save Ontario Shipwrecks, 43
Schaeffer, Edward, 75–76
Scourge: ghost of, 35, 44; renaming of,
    36, 37; shipwreck, 36, 43–44; storm
    and sinking of, 40–42; War of 1812,
    35, 37–42
Sea Serpent, Operation, 114
Serapis (Great Britain), 13
Seven Paranormal Research, 98
"Shadow Ed," 113, 115–16
Shannon (Great Britain), 31
ships: ghost fleet, 1, 29, 142–44;
    naming of after previous ships,

42, 107, 113, 116, 123; ships
as belonging to ghosts, 131;
superstitions aboard, 123
Showboat, 94. See also North Carolina
Sir John Sherbrooke (Nova Scotia), 32
Small, Elisha, 62–64
Somers: Africa voyage and mission, 57,
59–65; design of, 55–56; discipline
aboard, 59–60, 63–64; Mackenzie
as commander, 56, 57; Mexican
War duty, 66–68; mutinous plan
and executions to punish, 60–65;
reputation and haunting of, 65–69;
shipwreck, 68–69; sinking of, 68;
Spencer as officer, 57–59; as training
vessel, 56, 69; U.S. Naval Academy
birth from tragedy of, 69, 71
Somers, Richard, 55
"The Somers: A Ballad," 55, 63, 64–66,
68
Sophiasburg Triangle, 36
South China Sea, 113–14
Southeast Asian Treaty Organization,
114
Spain Revisited (Mackenzie), 56
Spellman, Francis J., 120
Spencer, John Canfield, 58, 65
Spencer, Philip: appearance and
character of, 58–59, 60; career of, 58,
59; mutinous plan and executions to
punish, 60–65; Somers assignment,
57–59
St. Lawrence (Great Britain), 38
Starboard Light, 84–85
Sterrett, Andrew, 20
Stewart, Donald, 24–25
Stick, Gordon M. F., 26–27
Stodder, David, 17
Sullivan, Al, 117–18, 119–20
Sullivan, Alleta Abel, 117, 119–20
Sullivan, Frank, 117–18, 119–20
Sullivan, Genevieve, 117
Sullivan, George, 117–18, 119–20
Sullivan, Joe, 117–18, 119–20

Sullivan, Matt, 117–18, 119–20
Sullivan, Thomas F., 117, 119–20
The Sullivans, 120–22
Superior, 38
Superior, Lake, 44
superstition, 123
Sutton, James N., Jr. "Jimmie":
Academy experience, 71; autopsy of,
76; death of, 70–71, 72–73; ghost of,
71, 72–73, 74, 76–77; investigation
into death, 73–76; Marine Corps
officer-training program, 71–72;
mother's bond with, 70; suicide and
Catholic Church, 73, 76
Sutton, Rosa Brant: ghost of Jimmie,
72–73, 74; investigation into
Jimmie's death, 73–76; Jimmie's
autopsy and Catholic Church, 76;
premonitions and telepathic bonds,
70, 72, 74–75

Tallmadge, Dorothy, 129
Teazer, 29–30
Tenedos (Great Britain), 31
Tennessee, 101
Texas: career of, 89–92; construction
of, 89; ghost of, 90, 93–94, 99;
museum status, 92–94, 99; nickname
of, 89; World War II role, 90–92
Thacher, M. A., 74
Tingey, Thomas, 78–79
Tingey House, 78–79
Tinian, 123
Tokyo Rose, 106
Tonkin Gulf, 138, 141
Tora! Tora! Tora!, 114
Torch, Operation, 91
Torpedo Squadron 8, 132
Tracy, Benjamin Franklin, 81–82
Tracy House, 81–82
Tripoli: Decatur's fight to avenge
brother's death, 47–48; Decatur's
treaty, 49; Philadelphia, 46; Somers
fate at, 55

Truxtun, Thomas, 17–18, 19, 25, 27, 28, 93
Tsushima battle ensign, 100, 101, 104
Tunis, 49
Tyler, John, 65

Unforgiven, 103–4
United Nations, World Heritage Sites, 43
United States, 49
University of Pittsburgh, Lynch Hall, 84–85
Upshur, Abel, 65
U.S. Army, 69
U.S. Fish and Wildlife Service, 104–5
U.S. Marine Corps: investigation into Sutton's death, 73–74, 75–76; Marine Corps Air Station Miramar, 137; officer-training program, 71–72
U.S. Naval Academy: acceptance at as honor, 71; Bancroft Hall, 14, 77; Carvel Hall, 72; ghosts at, 77; Halligan Hall, 71–72; Jones (John Paul) crypt, 14, 15–16; Jones (John Paul) ghost, 15–16, 77; Mahan Hall, 75; Marine Corps officer-training program, 71–72; opening of, 71; rigorous life at, 71; Somers tragedy and birth of, 69, 71; Sutton (James N., Jr.) ghost, 76–77; Sutton's death at, 70–71; West Point model of training, 69, 71
U.S. Naval Gun Factory, 79
U.S. Naval Postgraduate School, Monterey, 81
U.S. Naval Shipyard, Norfolk, 83
U.S. Naval Station Annapolis, 77
U.S. Naval Weapons Station, Yorktown, 82–83
U.S. Navy: ghost fleet, 1, 29, 142–44; haunted history of, 143; haunting of stations, 78, 83; Jones as father of, 13–14; privateers, 4–5, 6, 10, 29; vessels of, building, 17–18

U.S. Navy Department, 73–74, 75–76

Van Valkenburgh, Franklin, 100
La Vengeance (France), 20, 47
Veracruz, Battle of, 90
Vietnam War: Forrestal, 138–39, 141; Hornet, 124; Lexington, 109–10; Olathe Naval Air Station, 134; Oriskany, 136; Tonkin Gulf, 138, 141; Yorktown, 114

Wales, Steward James, 61
War of 1812: Chesapeake-Leopard affair, 48; Constellation, 20; Dash, 4–6; Decatur's actions, 49; ghost from, 83; Hamilton, 35, 37–38, 40, 41; Lake Ontario, 36; Scourge, 35, 37–42; shipbuilding during, 37–38; Teazer, 29–30; United States, 49; Young Teazer, 29, 30–34
Washington Naval Treaty, 94
Washington Navy Yard, 78–79
Webster, Neal R., 135
West Point, 69
West Virginia, 101
Western Gulf Blockading Squadron, 87
Wheeler, Susan, 48. See also Decatur, Susan Wheeler
When Ghosts Speak (Winkowski), 75
"White Lady of Rockingham," 14–15
Whittier, John Greenleaf, 8, 9
Wilson, Grant, 99
Winkowski, Mary Ann, 75
Woolsey, Commodore, 133
World Heritage Sites, 43
World War I: Pensacola Naval Air Station, 133; Texas role, 90
World War II: on Arizona, 100–101, 104; Arizona, 117; on Arizona, 117; Caroline Islands, 120; Casco Bay as most important seaport, 2–3; Cherbourg, Battle of, 91, 93; Constellation role, 22; Coral Sea,

Battle of the, 104, 107; Doolittle raid, 123, 124; fleet of the dead appearances, 2, 9; Flintlock, Operation, 113; Gilbert Islands, 113; Guadalcanal, 95, 118–19; Guam, 113, 116, 123; Henderson Field, 118; Hornet, 123–24; Iwo Jima, 91–92, 124; Juneau, 118–19, 121; Kwajalein, 109, 120; Lexington, 107–9, 113; Leyte Gulf, Battle of, 109, 124; Luzon, 109; Magic Carpet, Operation, 92; Mariana Islands, 109, 113, 120, 124; Marshall Islands, 113; Midway, Battle of, 104, 113, 116, 123, 132; North Carolina, 94–95; Okinawa, 92, 95, 114, 120, 124, 142; Ormoc Bay, 124; Palau Islands, 120; Pearl Harbor, 100–104, 114; Philippine Sea, Battle of the, 109, 113, 123; Rota, 123; Saipan, 113, 123; Santa Cruz Islands, Battle of, 123; South China Sea, 113–14; The Sullivans, 120–21; Texas role, 90–92; Tinian, 123; Torch, Operation, 91; Yorktown, 113–14

Yamato (Japan), 114, 124
Yankee Racehorse, 20. See also Constellation
A Year in Spain (Mackenzie), 56
Yemen Harbor, 143
York, Ontario, 38
Yorktown: ghosts of, 113, 115–16; launching of, 113; museum status, 114–16; naming of, 113; nickname of, 113; post-World War II career, 114; sinking of ships with same name, 113, 116; sister ships, 113, 124; Vietnam War role, 114; World War II role, 113–14
Young Teazer, 29–34

About the Author

Eric Mills is the author of *Chesapeake Bay in the Civil War* and *Chesapeake Rumrunners of the Roaring Twenties*. His articles have appeared in *Naval History*, *Proceedings*, *Chesapeake Bay Magazine*, and other publications. A longtime devotee of both sea history and ghostly phenomena, he lives in Maryland.

The **Naval Institute Press** is the book-publishing arm of the U.S. Naval Institute, a private, nonprofit, membership society for sea service professionals and others who share an interest in naval and maritime affairs. Established in 1873 at the U.S. Naval Academy in Annapolis, Maryland, where its offices remain today, the Naval Institute has members worldwide.

Members of the Naval Institute support the education programs of the society and receive the influential monthly magazine *Proceedings* or the colorful bimonthly magazine *Naval History* and discounts on fine nautical prints and on ship and aircraft photos. They also have access to the transcripts of the Institute's Oral History Program and get discounted admission to any of the Institute-sponsored seminars offered around the country.

The Naval Institute's book-publishing program, begun in 1898 with basic guides to naval practices, has broadened its scope to include books of more general interest. Now the Naval Institute Press publishes about seventy titles each year, ranging from how-to books on boating and navigation to battle histories, biographies, ship and aircraft guides, and novels. Institute members receive significant discounts on the Press's more than eight hundred books in print.

Full-time students are eligible for special half-price membership rates. Life memberships are also available.

For a free catalog describing Naval Institute Press books currently available, and for further information about joining the U.S. Naval Institute, please write to:

Member Services
U.S. Naval Institute
291 Wood Road
Annapolis, MD 21402-5034
Telephone: (800) 233-8764
Fax: (410) 571-1703
Web address: www.usni.org